Nest Quest ROI

An Engine & Simulator to Outrun Interest and Resist Inflation

Mohammed Billah

Nest Quest ROI: An Engine and Simulator

INVESTED AMOUNT	**INTEREST RATE**	**PROPERTY TAX RATE**	**SELL COMMISSION**	**MAINTENANCE COST**
$300K	**6%**	**2%**	**6%**	**8%**

TERM	**ASSET APPRECIATION**	**RENT GROWTH RATE**	**GOLD APPRECIATION RATE**	**RTO EQUITY SPLIT**
20 Years	**5%**	**2%**	**8.8%**	**46% Rent / 57% Equity**

INVESTMENT OUTCOMES

RTO	RTO+ Gold	Traditional Rent	Bank Lending
ROI 67%	**ROI 236%**	**ROI 224%**	**ROI 58%**
IRR 2.75%	IRR 6.6%	IRR 6.1%	IRR 2.33%
$200K	$700K	$673K	$175K
19y	19y	20y	20y

Investment Strategy Comparison – $300k over 20-year base term

RTO models exited in 18.9 years based on performance

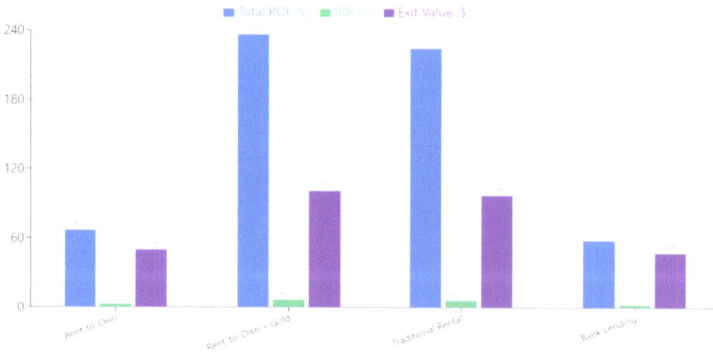

2

NestQuestROI

Gold never leaves the throne. Real estate doesn't retire.
Together, they don't just grow wealth — they multiply it.

Nest Quest ROI

Nest Quest ROI: An Engine & Simulator to Outrun Interest and Resist Inflation were independently developed as both a research-grade book and a live simulator. Its models, methods, and figures originate from the author, with diagrams drawn from primary sources. Built on a single-ledger method, it allows households to see lifetime costs, pace of ownership, and clean exit options; operators weigh hold, renovate, or reposition under the same rules; lenders and investors compare products on outcomes, not brochures; and researchers, educators, and institutions run results, stress inputs, and build coursework or policy tests using a shared, auditable method.

Learn the system, compare the trade-offs, and choose with clarity; then use the engine to pursue outcomes that outrun interest and resist inflation.

Nest Quest ROI unites destination, journey, and discipline across time. *Nest* is the present, the home, and the reality you live in today. *Quest* is a solid, step-by-step plan through a real maze: rent, mortgage, buy, or rent-to-own, while staying ahead of headwinds such as interest and inflation that quietly make families lose ground. *ROI* is the future that you are building toward; the return that proves the path is worth it. Lessons from the past act as guardrails, the present sets inputs, and the aim is a better future. The book and simulator turn this promise into practice by replaying history, setting today's numbers, and testing tomorrow's outcomes under the same rules. One destination, a navigable quest, and choices are guided by the ROI.

First Edition, 2025

Publisher: SoftTelRG Press (Texas, USA)

ISBN (E-Book): 979-8-9930977-0-1
ISBN (Hardback): 979-8-9930977-1-8
ISBN (Paperback): 979-8-9930977-2-5
ISBN (Hardcover with Dust Jacket): 979-8-9930977-3-2
Library of Congress Control Number (LCCN): 2025919393

Cover & Interior Design: SoftTelRG Press

Developmental Editing: Farida Yesmin
Copyediting: Farida Yesmin
Proofreading: Farida Yesmin

Data and Reproducibility: Methods and parameter blocks appear in the front matter and at NestQuestROI.com. The figures are reproducible using a simulator.

Dedication

To Yesmin

Your faith and thoughtful editorial eye give this book its spine.

You turn midnight into morning with coffee and patience.

You ask the right questions, and the pages make sense.

If anything shines here, it is your light.

Acknowledgments

All thanks to Almighty for this opportunity.

To my better half, the first reviewer and constant influence. You asked difficult questions, cut off the fluff and insisted on clarity.

To my little angel and parents, whose love and support have guided me at every step.

To my family and in-laws, whose encouragement and devotion have made every challenge worth it.

To the researchers and engineers who tested the simulator.

Early readers and the global community of practitioners and scholars whose critiques have made this book tighter and more useful.

Abstract

Nest Quest ROI is both a **research-grade book** and **live, auditable simulator**. It introduces a universal **single-ledger engine** that rigorously models and compares all major housing and lending pathways–rent, mortgage, rent-to-own, and hybrid contracts–using both nominal and inflation-adjusted (CPI-U deflated) terms.

Its originality rests on four breakthroughs.

1. **Live Simulator**: A continuously updated, user-driven engine where households, lenders, investors, operators, and policymakers input real-time market data, rates, rents, and inflation, and evaluate outcomes with identical assumptions. This transforms the work into a dynamic *living laboratory*.

2. **Innovative Metrics (RNIM & ERA)**: Defines **Real Net Interest Margin (RNIM)** and **Equity Return on Asset (ERA)** as precise measures of real economic performance, revealing hidden structural costs and overlooked margin opportunities.

3. **Mathematical Proof of Institutional Benefit**: Formal ledger math proves that institutions can sustainably enhance profitability and resilience by adopting transparent allocation contracts (e.g., rent-to-own structures).

4. **Digital Gold Savings Account (DGSA)**: Proposes a policy-compatible, inflation-resilient savings rail that records balances in both local currency and gold grams, preserving household savings without undermining the monetary policy.

Reproducibility by design ensures that every figure is paired with parameter blocks and ruleset hashes, enabling transparent replication and extension on **NestQuestROI.com**.

Multi-stakeholder value
- **Households**: Transparent, inflation-aware, rent-vs-buy clarity.
- **Lenders/Investors**: Real-margin measurement and resilient contract design.
- **Operators**: Unified testing of investment and repositioning options.

- **Policymakers**: Pilot-governed, non-disruptive ownership alternatives.
- **Innovators/Fintechs**: Open models for new ventures with verified mathematics.

Summary: *Nest Quest ROI* is not merely a book. It is a **prototype financial architecture**: a live simulator, mathematical proof system, and set of policy-neutral innovations that empower households, institutions, and regulators to achieve ownership and savings outcomes that consistently **outrun interest and resist inflation**.

Review

We welcome formal peer review, but we are not unduly concerned about biased or influenced judgments because the Nest Quest ROI is already designed for continuous public verification. Every model, proof, and figure is linked to explicit parameter blocks, version hashes, and a live simulator at NestQuestROI.com, allowing any reader, scholar, policymaker, practitioner, or household to independently reproduce and cross-check the results. Unless the platform is deliberately hacked or suppressed for external interests, transparency functions as an open and ongoing peer review by the global public.

Peer-Review & Reproducibility Checklist

- Parameter blocks: Each figure/table includes a parameter block and a short ruleset hash.
- CPI basis: CPI-U (U.S. City Average). The real values are the deflated CPI-U (index method) values.
- Day count and IRR: Annual effective IRR; Actual/Actual day-count.
- Funding and costs: Explicit costs of funds, operating expenses, and expected losses, where applicable.
- Sensitivity: One-at-a-time unless stated; ±0.5–2.0 p.p. bands on key rates.
- Provenance: Series IDs and date windows are cited; exports include parameters and ruleset hashes.
- Replication: Scenarios can be rerun at NestQuestROI.com using the posted parameter block.

Ethics and Disclosure

No sponsored research or third-party funding was used to determine the models or conclusions. The code and assumptions are disclosed to the extent permitted by law. The author is the creator of the Nest Quest ROI engine and simulator; no external sponsorship or compensation influenced the analysis.

Accessibility Statement

The eBook is optimized for reflowable text, bookmarks, alternative text in figures, and high-contrast palettes. Print editions use readable Serif types and accessible figure labels.

How to Cite This Book

APA: Billah, M. (2025). *Nest Quest ROI: An Engine & Simulator to Outrun Interest and Resist Inflation*. SoftTelRG Press.

Chicago: Billah, Mohammed. *Nest Quest ROI: An Engine & Simulator to Outrun Interest and Resist Inflation*. Texas: SoftTelRG Press, 2025.

NestQuestROI.com

Contents

Preface

Nearly every household in the world shares a simple dream: owning a home. It is not just a place to live but also a symbol of dignity, security, and legacy for the next generation. However, beneath that simple dream lies a silent struggle: the cost of owning anything–a house, business, or even peace of mind–is rising faster than most people can keep up.

Inflation reduces purchasing power, and interest increases overall ownership. The combination lengthens the time-to-goal for many households, not because of insufficient effort but because the rules price time unevenly.

That weight, the drag of inflation, and the cost of interest do not care about who you are or where you live. Business owners or workers, parents or students are all pulled by the same invisible hands. This dream of ownership fuels housing markets, drives national policy, and fills global banks' balance sheets. However, what if the system behind that dream is also the reason why so many people never achieve it?

This book is for those who have felt friction: everyday families, solo entrepreneurs, thoughtful investors, and policymakers seeking something better. This explains why interest-based finance and rent-dependent systems often work against us, even when we play by the rules of the game. More importantly, it offers a different path, one rooted in shared values, earned equity, and smarter and safer reinvestments.

In the United States, over 44 million households (~ 35%) live in rental housing (According to the ACS 1-year 2023 Table B25003, the U.S. had 45,646,491 renter-occupied- households out of 131,332,360 occupied units (~34.8%)). Annual tenant-occupied rent flows exceed $500 billion (Bureau of Economic Analysis, NIPA Table 2.4.5U, 2023). Meanwhile, approximately 62% of homes carry mortgages (U.S. Census Bureau, ACS Table B25081, 2023). Globally, estimates exceed 1 billion renters, and residential real estate is valued at approximately $250 trillion (Savills Research 2020; 2023 update $379.7T at end-2022).

These numbers show greater dependency than market activity. They reflect a world where most people either rent what they will never own or borrow money they can barely afford to repay. Beyond homes, there is an even larger layer of interest-based property financing that often goes unnoticed: commercial buildings, corporate campuses, factories, warehouses, and infrastructure such as toll roads and energy facilities, many of which are financed through complex long-term debt instruments backed by banks or government bonds. If we include these properties, the scale of the interest-based property system becomes even more staggering, with tens of trillions of dollars tied up in long-term liabilities, exposing not only households but also entire industries to systemic financial risk. In fact, entire cities, such as Detroit in 2013, filed for bankruptcy due in part to unsustainable debt structures linked to real estate obligations, pension liabilities, and financial mismanagement (In re City of Detroit, Michigan, Case No. 13-53846 (Bankr. E.D. Mich. 2013), Chapter 9 Bankruptcy Filing Summary). When cities collapse financially, the effects ripple through the housing markets, municipal services, and job security. Again, the following question arises: Where is the real protection for the public in this scenario? During crises, authorities deploy extraordinary measures, such as TARP authorizations in 2008 and a 2023 systemic-risk exception for uninsured deposits at specific institutions. While the mechanics differ (capital backstops vs. deposit guarantees), the distributional question remains: which stakeholders absorb losses and which are shielded by policy? This book does not litigate these choices; rather, it examines their distributional effects and tests the alternatives they govern.

Prevailing accounts characterize interest- and rent-based systems as the backbone of modern finance, largely because they were protected by the Federal Reserve and global central banks during major crises. These central bank interventions reinforce the perception that these systems are essential for maintaining economic stability. However, when the same bailout patterns are repeated and shielding institutions while everyday citizens absorb the cost, it is fair to question whether these models truly serve the public interest.

To explore this question, this book is structured in three parts.
- Part One: Learn how the system works and identify challenges.
- Part Two: Finding the gaps in the system.
- Part Three: Provide solutions and validate with the Nest Quest ROI.

If you wonder why so many people work hard yet still feel stuck, you are not alone. This book evaluates distributional outcomes across lending and ownership models and tests complementary mechanisms under similar assumptions.

Real-World Challenges in Banking, Finance, and Real Estate.
Conventional wisdom states that banks and mortgages are safe and landlords make easy money; however, a closer look at the ledger shows recurring gaps.
- Rental margins shrink once maintenance, capital repairs, taxes, insurance, management, and vacancies are fully counted.
- Aging increases costs faster than rent, compressing cash flow unless reinvestment is planned and funded accordingly.
- Renters often complete long payment periods without ownership claims.
- Lenders' real returns are fragile because inflation lowers the value of interest income and refinancing or funding costs compress spreads.
- Nominal gains can be misleading, and we evaluate the results in inflation-adjusted terms to determine the true performance.

The Gap Between Earning and Growing. This section identifies three structural frictions that prevent income from compounding into durable wealth:
- Idle cash drag: Low-yield balances lose purchasing power in real (inflation-adjusted) terms.
- Access and visibility gaps: Without a basic liquidity ladder, funds are either idle or chase undisciplined risk.
- Infrastructure mismatch: Widely trusted stores of value (e.g., gold) remain weakly integrated with mainstream rails; thus, long-horizon preservation sits outside everyday finance.

Turning Payments into Equity That Grows Ahead of Inflation and Interest. It presents a single-ledger framework that converts payments into equity and tests preservation and growth policies in CPI-adjusted terms, with identical inputs.

- Engine and simulator: One ledger, identical inputs, nominal and CPI-adjusted outputs, and parameter hashes were used for replication.
- Rent-to-own contract: Payments are allocated to use, equity credit, and operating costs with defined maintenance gates, hardship reversion, and exit waterfalls.
- Digital Gold Savings Account (DGSA): Policy-neutral preservation rail, currency and gram balances, and standard taxation and reporting.
- RTO plus reinvestment: Side-by-side with RTO+Gold and RTO+Stock to show when preservation and growth balance and when each underperforms.
- Banks, operators, investors, and individual pathways are included. Implementation checklists, model governance, transparent communication, and stop rules.

Replication and access: All comparative scenarios in this book can be reproduced at www.NestQuestROI.com using identical input and export settings.

- Compare financial models side by side, rent vs. mortgage vs. RTO + Gold or RTO + Stock
- Track projected wealth growth for both tenants and investors
- Understand how gold-backed or stock-based savings resist inflation and preserve value

Data Sources. All statistics cited are based on publicly available reports from sources, including the U.S. Census Bureau, Federal Reserve, OECD, and others. Where applicable, proprietary data were paraphrased and attributed to the original sources.

Thoughts. The financial system is already in motion; the engine is running, and the wheels are turning. This book does not ask to rebuild the engine. It simply offers a bit of oil to help the wheels spin more smoothly.

This book does not propose replacing the existing financial architecture. It documents how it operates, where it compresses real outcomes for households and institutions, and which complementary mechanisms can improve resilience without disrupting the monetary policy or market structure. The goal is incremental, testable refinement, implemented through transparent contracts (RTO), inflation-resilient savings (DGSA), and an auditable simulator (Nest Quest ROI) that allows any stakeholder to validate results with their own assumptions.

Note: This book is an educational analysis using reproducible methods; it does not provide investment, legal or tax advice. Readers should apply local rules and consult qualified advisors, where appropriate.

Methods 1.1: Common Methods and Assumptions: All figures are in USD; real values deflate the nominal series by CPI-U (index method), with real growth approximated as nominal minus CPI when acceptable. IRR uses annual effective rates with actual/actual day-count; baseline loans are fixed-rate, fully amortizing; taxes/insurance/fees are modeled on a cash basis (origination at t=0); baseline CPR = 0 with variants labeled. Sensitivities are one-at-a-time unless noted (rates ±0.5–2.0 p.p.; p.p. = percentage points); time-sensitive values are cited as series, with replication at www.NestQuestROI.com (Methods and Data). Unless otherwise noted, *real* values are CPI-U–deflated; RNIM is expressed in annual percentage points; all return 'ranges' are illustrative and period dependent.

Part One

Real-World Challenges in Banking, Finance, and Real Estate

Chapter 1
Mechanics of Modern Lending

Modern finance touches nearly every part of life, from the homes that households live in to the buildings that firms occupy and the infrastructure that connects them. However, the underlying mechanics have rarely been examined beyond the headline rates and monthly payments. This chapter describes the mechanics at the system level. It begins with two canonical loops, the mortgage cycle and the business lending cycle, to show how cash, claims, and risk move through public institutions, private intermediaries, and households.

On the surface, both loops appear to be engines of growth. Tracing cash flows reveals recurrent patterns in how senior claims are prioritized, risk is transferred, and repayments interact with public backstops and private reinvestment.

Scenario 1: The Mortgage Loop: When Public Money Supports Private Credit. This architecture relies on public trust and the law. How it works:

- Public issuance. The U.S. Treasury issues bills, notes, and bonds that investors purchase. In specific programs, the Federal Reserve may buy treasuries and, in some programs, agency MBS, affecting market yields and bank reserves [2].
- Bank balance sheets. Banks manage capital, liquidity, and funding costs while extending mortgages, and reserve balances earn the administered Interest on Reserve Balances (IORB) [3].
- Origination and sale. Lenders issue mortgages at prevailing market rates and often securitize them into agency pools to conform loans. Servicing rights and fees arise at this stage [4,6].
- Monthly outlays. Borrowers remit the principal and interest; escrow commonly covers property taxes and homeowners insurance; and closing or servicing fees remunerate intermediaries.

- Cash-flow distribution. Interest and servicing income accrue to lenders or servicers, property tax flows support local budgets, and principal amortization reduces borrower debt.
- Stress episodes. In liquidity stress or market dysfunction, lenders and markets may access central bank facilities (e.g., repo operations and historical QE episodes) and statutory backstops; deposit insurance protects retail deposits [2,5,7, 9].

Observation: The public sector underwrites key layers (central bank money or reserves, deposit insurance, and liquidity facilities), whereas most transactions are settled in bank deposits and private liabilities that are convertible into legal tender. Multiple parties hold senior claims (contractually prior claims on cash flows, interest or fees, paid before residual equity) on the borrower's payment stream; the borrower's residual depends on time and asset performance. This is by design and not by accident.

Scenario 2: The Business Loan Loop: When Growth Brings Its Own Cost Pressures. Small and medium-sized firms borrow to fund their working capital, equipment, and expansion. Funding is drawn from the same system of deposits, capital markets, and bank balance sheets that support household credit. Once borrowed, the obligation to provide service debt shapes a firm's pricing and cost decisions. How it works:
- Credit demand: A firm secures a term loan or revolving facility at the market rate by pledging collateral and/or a guarantee.
- Operating response: To meet the fixed debt service, the firm seeks higher margins through productivity gains, cost controls, and, where market power allows price increases.
- Price dynamics: Under capacity constraints or strong demand, these adjustments can contribute to the price pressures observed in consumer or producer price indices (illustrative: identification is empirical, not mechanical) [8]. Causal attribution requires identification (e.g., such as instruments or panel methods). We treat these channels as testable and not assumed (see Methods 1.2).

- Feedback. Higher input costs and wages compress margins, prompting further adjustments, expense controls, deferred investments, or additional credit.
- Payoff profile. Lenders earn interest regardless of the project outcome; in the case of failure, collateral is realized and residual losses are recognized.

Observation: Credit enables investment, but repayment prioritizes the first channel of cash to senior claims. The distribution of gains and losses depends on the market power, productivity, and timing. Here, the inflation dynamics are conditional and empirical, not automatic in nature.

Shared Architecture Across Lending Loops
- Common funding base. Both loops rely directly or indirectly on publicly supported monetary and legal infrastructure and private funding markets.
- Interest-based seniority: Repayment schedules prioritize interests and fees and establish senior claims over residual equity.
- Stability through obligation: Systemic stability is achieved by distributing obligations across many borrowers while centralizing backstops.
- Directional flow: In the absence of appreciation or retained earnings, capital circulates forward through institutions and does not necessarily cycle back to the original borrowers.

These are architectural features and not anomalies.

The Capital Loop: Funding, Liquidity and Reinvestment. Banks do not rely solely on retail deposits. They manage a stack of funding sources (core deposits, term deposits, secured and unsecured wholesale funding), capital constraints, liquidity requirements, and interest rate and duration risks. During times of stress, institutions may have access to central bank liquidity facilities or capital markets. Once the loans are in the book, interest income and fees arrive as cash flow. Cash is not static: a portion supports operations and regulatory buffers; the remainder is redeployed into new credit, government and agency securities, or other permissible assets in line with the mandate and risk appetite [6].

Therefore, the loop closes in repayment but remains open in reinvestment. Borrower cash flow services, senior claims, and institutional cash flows are redeployed. The loan ends, and the capital keeps moving.

Implications. We mapped how payments, claims, and backstops moved through the current system. However, this does not establish whether a contractual promise of ownership was achieved. Chapter 2 examines ownership in practice, including definitions, claim priority, pacing of equity, and the allocation of time and risk across contracts.

Methods and Data: All quantitative illustrations in Part 1 use public series (e.g., BLS CPI-U), bank segment disclosures, and standard loan/bond mathematics [1,6,8]. IRR conventions follow the stated assumptions; real values are deflated by CPI-U. Scenario tables and sensitivity analyses can be reproduced using the same inputs and export settings posted at ***www.NestQuestROI.com*** *(Methods and Data).*

Methods 1.2: Identification Note: Chapter 1 is descriptive: price effects are testable channels, not assumptions, and face simultaneity, selection, reverse causality, and omitted-variable risks. Credible evidence relies on IV, panel FE/DiD, event studies, or cost-shock pass-through with robust errors and pre-trend checks; no causal coefficients are estimated.

Endnotes

[1] Methods & Definitions. Brealey, Myers, Allen (2020), Principles of Corporate Finance, 13e.
[2] QE/Program Mechanics. FRBNY LSAPs – program archive.
[3] Administered Rate / IORB. Board of Governors, Interest on Reserve Balances,
[4] Mortgage Rates (prevailing). Freddie Mac Primary Mortgage Market Survey (PMMS). Agency guarantees and securitization: Fannie Mae/Freddie Mac (GSE guarantees), Ginnie Mae (full faith and credit; FHA/VA/USDA collateral). Non-agency MBS lack explicit or implicit government credit support.
[5] Repo Operations (example episode). FRBNY market notices, September 2019.
[6] Bank income/NIM/servicing context. FDIC (2025), Quarterly Banking Profile – Q1 2025; FFIEC Call Reports.
[7] Deposit Insurance. FDIC, Deposit Insurance – Overview. Legal tender in the U.S. refers to currency and coins (e.g., Federal Reserve notes). Bank deposits are private liabilities, widely used for settlement and convertible at par into central-bank money by eligible institutions
[8] Inflation Series. BLS CPI-U, U.S. City Average (Table 1).
[9] TARP Backstop (example). U.S. Treasury, Office of Financial Stability, TARP Programs and Investments.
[10] Microcredit Evidence (RCT cluster). Banerjee et al. (2015), Karlan & Zinman (2011), Roodman & Morduch (2014).

Chapter 2

Conditional Ownership

Definition 2.1 — Rent-to-Price Heuristic (1/180): Use 1/180 as an orientation, not a rule: monthly rent ≈ purchase price ÷ 180 (≈ gross rent multiplied by 15). We report this empirically using the Metropolitan Statistical Area (MSA), showing the median, interquartile range, and minimum and maximum over a fixed window (e.g., 2015–2025), and display the full distribution (density plot) for transparency. Rents are pinned to the Zillow Observed Rent Index (ZORI) methodology (asking-rent series) and cross-checked against the U.S. Census American Community Survey (ACS) Tables B25058 (Median Contract Rent) and B25077 (Median Home Value); outliers are winsorized at conventional tails; methods are documented in the Methods and Data section. This heuristic only initializes scenarios; all underwriting uses local operating costs, financing terms, and observed rent levels, rather than the ratio itself. [11,12]

Ownership is widely treated as the finish line: stability, equity, and something to pass on. In modern finance, most ownership is purchased through debt. The title may be in the buyer's name, but the control is conditional until the senior claims are satisfied. Taxes, insurance, and debt services are paid before the owner participates in any surplus. If you miss enough payments, the contract tells you what happens next: late fees, acceleration, and, if unresolved, the loss of assets. This is not a flaw in the system; it is how interest-based credit is built.

What "conditional" looks like month to month. The monthly sheet determines who is truly in charge. If the net operating income after ordinary costs (property taxes, insurance, maintenance, management, and typical vacancy) are lower than the mortgage payment, the owner must add cash to hold the keys. Many markets are priced such that new buyers start in a negative-carry position unless the rents are already high or the down payment is large. Mortgage rates and insurance/tax resets can push a borderline case into a cash drain, even when tenants pay on time. [4,6]

Why headline returns can mislead. Reported returns can appear strong at the end because leverage magnifies whatever happens to the price. If the property rises in value and sells in a good market, the sale proceeds can overwhelm the years of weak or negative cash flow. This does not mean that the asset was a steady earner; rather it means that the outcome depended on appreciation and timing. The best practice is to report both nominal and real IRR (CPI-U-deflated) and show exit-year sensitivities (e.g., 7, 10, 15, and 20 years). *See Methods 1.1.*

A 20-year illustration. Consider an investor who puts $300,000 down and finances $900,000 for a $1.2 million purchase. Over 20 years, the gross rent sums to roughly $2.7 million. Ordinary costs, including taxes, insurance, maintenance, management, and vacancy, plus interest, amounted to more than $3.0 million, and the $900,000 principal was repaid from the same cash flow. The running total is the negative cash flow (approximately $380,000 over the hold) that the owner had to cover from external income. The final outcome depends on the sale: if the property sells for around $3.0 million, the spreadsheet shows a large equity figure and an eye-catching return, driven mainly by appreciation and leverage, not by steady income. If the sales year or price path changes, the picture changes rapidly. The lesson is simple: owning debt often means funding losses in exchange for a hoped-for exit in the future. (All figures are illustrative; inputs and exact schedules are posted in Methods and Data.) [1,4,5,6]

The drag that owners actually feel: Three forces explain why many owners feel pressured, even during normal times.
- First, maintenance and vacancies were combined. Roofs, heating, ventilation, air conditioning (HVAC), and plumbing fail on their own schedule and not on the pro forma. A single vacant month wipes out that month's rent, while taxes, insurance, and mortgages still go out.
- Second, the non-operating line items can jump significantly. Reassessments can increase property taxes, and insurance premiums can be reset after severe weather or market repricing. These were not under the owners' control.
- Third, financing sets a pecking order. The lender's claim precedes the owner's claim. If debt services, even temporarily, outrun the property's ability to earn, the owner must bridge the gap or risk breaching the contract. In a tight credit window, refinancing may require new cash or sales at inappropriate times. [4,6]

The same logic applies to businesses. The structure is identical for all the business owners. Loans and leases were paid before distribution. When demand softens or input costs increase, the firm must raise prices, cut costs, or contribute outside cash to keep the covenants whole. Credit magnifies the success and consequences of ordinary volatility. Whether the asset is a house, duplex, or a storefront, senior claims are paid first.

Becoming an owner through an interest-based loan is not the same as outright ownership. It is a contract that allows users to use an asset while gradually buying senior claims. The system works as designed: lenders earn interest and fees on schedule, and owners participate in what remains. Sustainable ownership requires one of three types of support: strong operating income, conservative leverage, or patience backed by outside cash. Without at least one of these three, the model leans on appreciation and exit timing, which is a contingent strategy dependent on appreciation and exit timing.

Implications. Once ownership is defined in practice, the next step is determining the context. Chapter 3 maps the ecosystem, capital markets, public backstops, and regulations that channel funding and reallocate risks across institutions and households.

Methods and Data. All figures are expressed in U.S. dollars. Inflation adjustments are made using the Bureau of Labor Statistics Consumer Price Index for All Urban Consumers (CPI-U); the real IRR is computed as the IRR of the CPI-deflated cash flows. Mortgage rates are taken from Freddie Mac's Primary Mortgage Market Survey (PMMS); when scenarios assume fixed-rate, fully amortizing loans, this is stated; any departures (interest-only periods, balloons) are labeled in the table's notes. Operating items, such as property taxes, insurance, maintenance, management, and typical vacancies, are modeled on a cash basis in the period in which they occur; sale proceeds net standard transaction costs (assumption disclosed). Bank and servicing contexts follow FDIC Quarterly Banking Profile conventions, and the housing series follows ZORI and ACS (B25058, B25077). Each table specifies the data window, parameter choices, and sell-year sensitivity (Years 7/10/15/20); inputs, calculation sheets, and exports are posted at www.NestQuestROI.com (Methods and Data) for replication. [1,4,5,6,11,12]

Endnotes

[1] Methods & Definitions. Brealey, Myers, Allen (2020), Principles of Corporate Finance, 13e.

[4] Mortgage Rates (prevailing). Freddie Mac Primary Mortgage Market Survey (PMMS).

[5] Inflation Series. U.S. Bureau of Labor Statistics, CPI-U (U.S. City Average, Table 1).

[6] Bank income/servicing context. FDIC (2025), Quarterly Banking Profile – Q1 2025; FFIEC Call Reports.

[11] Zillow Research. Zillow Observed Rent Index (ZORI) methodology (asking-rent series).

[12] U.S. Census Bureau. American Community Survey: B25058 (Median Contract Rent) and B25077 (Median Home Value).

Chapter 3
The Financial Ecosystem

Modern money does not travel in a straight line. It is created on public balance sheets, multiplied by banks and markets, routed through payment rails, and partially drained by interest, taxes, and portfolio choices. The result is a public–private stack that makes interest-based ownership feasible and conditional by design.

The U.S. financial ecosystem runs in four tiers: (1) money creation and settlement (Treasury–Fed–banks), (2) credit multiplication (bank and market intermediation), (3) real-economy circulation (income, payments, deposit turnover), and (4) value drains and recycling (interest, taxes, and portfolio flows).

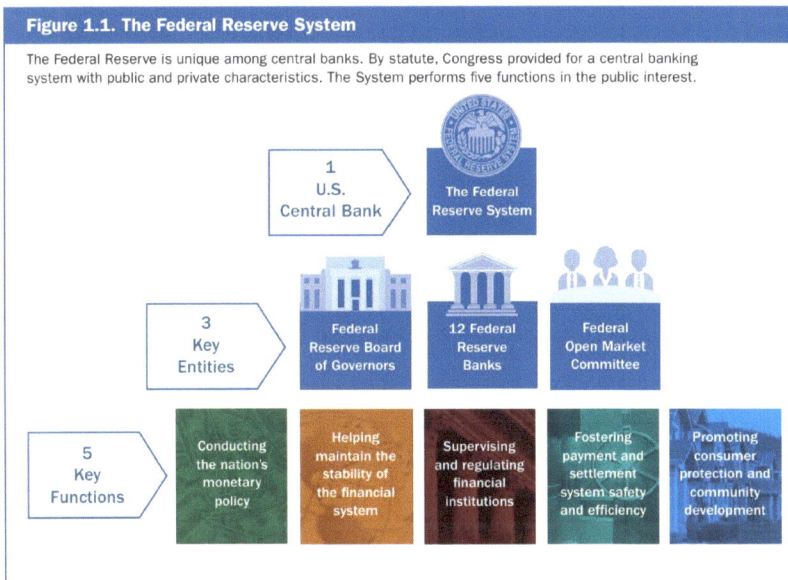

Figure 1.1. The Federal Reserve System

The Federal Reserve is unique among central banks. By statute, Congress provided for a central banking system with public and private characteristics. The System performs five functions in the public interest.

NestQuestROI.com

Figure 1.2. Three key entities, serving the public interest

The framers of the Federal Reserve Act developed a central banking system that would broadly represent the public interest.

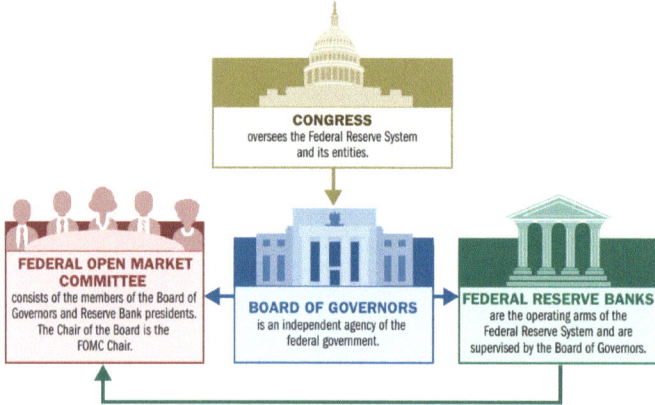

CONGRESS oversees the Federal Reserve System and its entities.

FEDERAL OPEN MARKET COMMITTEE consists of the members of the Board of Governors and Reserve Bank presidents. The Chair of the Board is the FOMC Chair.

BOARD OF GOVERNORS is an independent agency of the federal government.

FEDERAL RESERVE BANKS are the operating arms of the Federal Reserve System and are supervised by the Board of Governors.

Figure 4.1. The financial system: key participants and linkages

Key participants in the U.S. and global financial system include the lenders and savers who are matched up with borrowers and spenders through various markets and intermediaries. The Federal Reserve monitors the financial system to ensure the linkages among entities are well-functioning and adjusts its policymaking or engagement with other policymakers to address any emerging concerns.

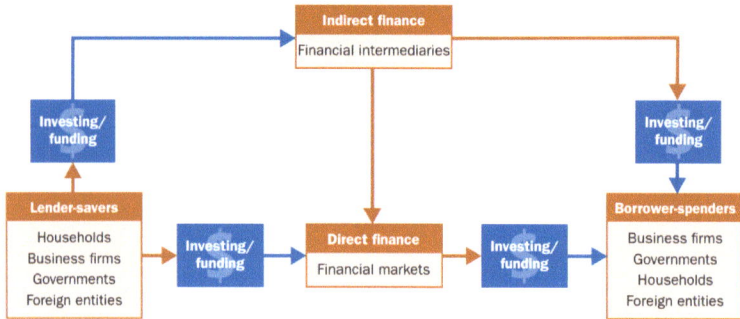

Indirect finance — Financial intermediaries

Investing/funding

Lender-savers
Households
Business firms
Governments
Foreign entities

Direct finance — Financial markets

Borrower-spenders
Business firms
Governments
Households
Foreign entities

Source: Adapted from Frederic S. Mishkin and Stanley G. Eakins, *Financial Markets and Institutions*. 7th Edition (Boston: Prentice Hall, 2012), 16.

32

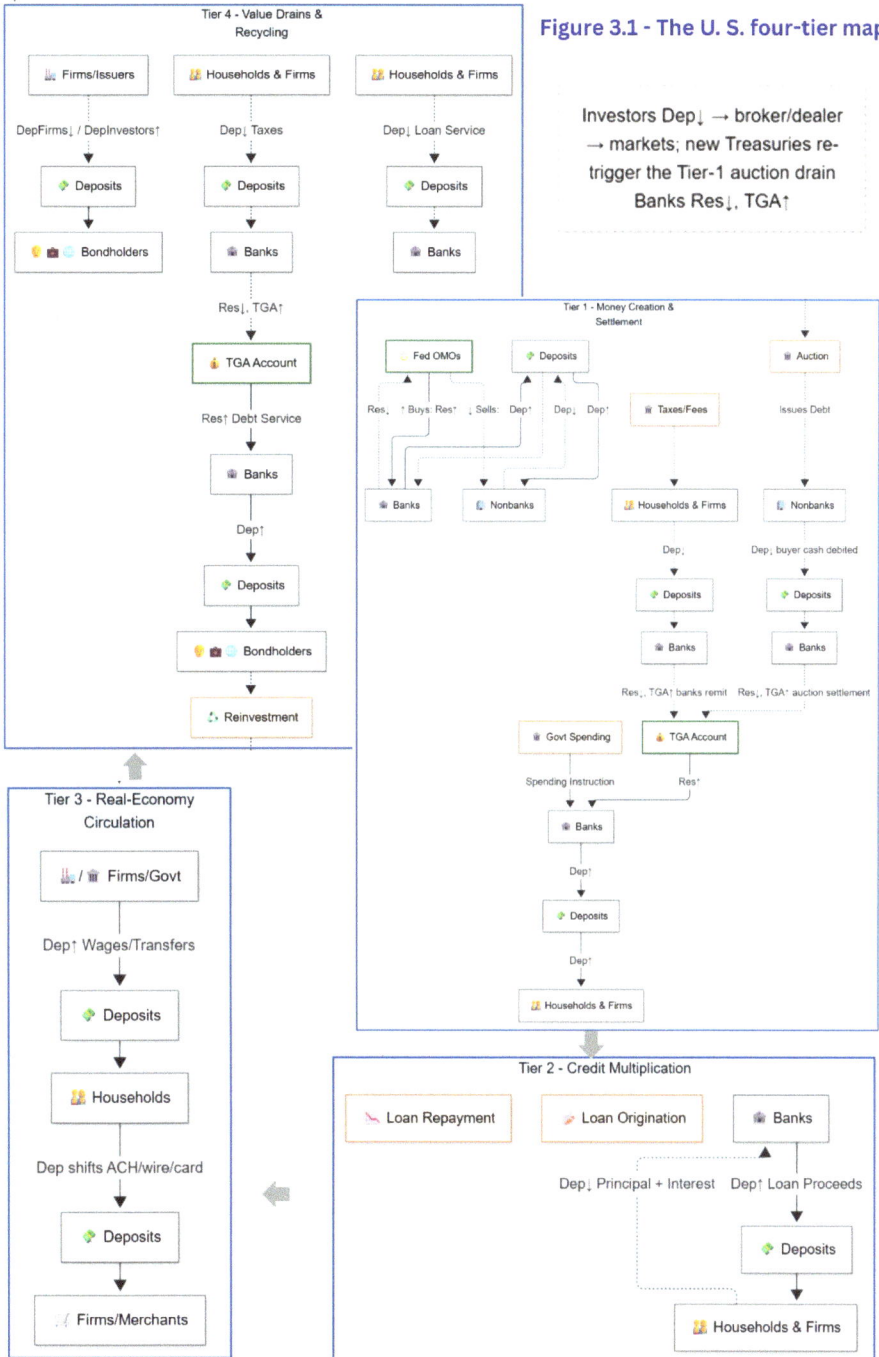

Figure 3.1 - The U. S. four-tier map

Investors Dep↓ → broker/dealer → markets; new Treasuries re-trigger the Tier-1 auction drain Banks Res↓, TGA↑

33

Figure 5.1. How the regulation and supervision process works

When Congress passes a law that impacts the financial industry, the Federal Reserve—sometimes in cooperation with other federal agencies—often issues regulations that determine how the law will be implemented.

REGULATION

CONGRESS votes to approve legislation; President signs into law → **FEDERAL RESERVE BOARD** drafts, proposes, and invites public comment on regulations that specify how laws are implemented → **AMERICAN PUBLIC** institutions, individuals, and others review proposed regulations and respond with comments and suggestions → **FEDERAL RESERVE BOARD** considers public input, finalizes regulations, and issues and disseminates final regulations publicly, including rationale for actions

SUPERVISION

REGULATED INSTITUTIONS implement internal practices to ensure that they are in compliance with regulations ← **FEDERAL RESERVE EXAMINERS** conduct on- and off-site examinations/inspections of regulated institutions to determine their compliance with regulations ← **FEDERAL RESERVE BANKS** train examiners to evaluate institutions' compliance with regulations ← **FEDERAL RESERVE BOARD** issues and disseminates publicly the procedures Reserve Bank examiners will use to evaluate institutions' compliance with laws and regulations

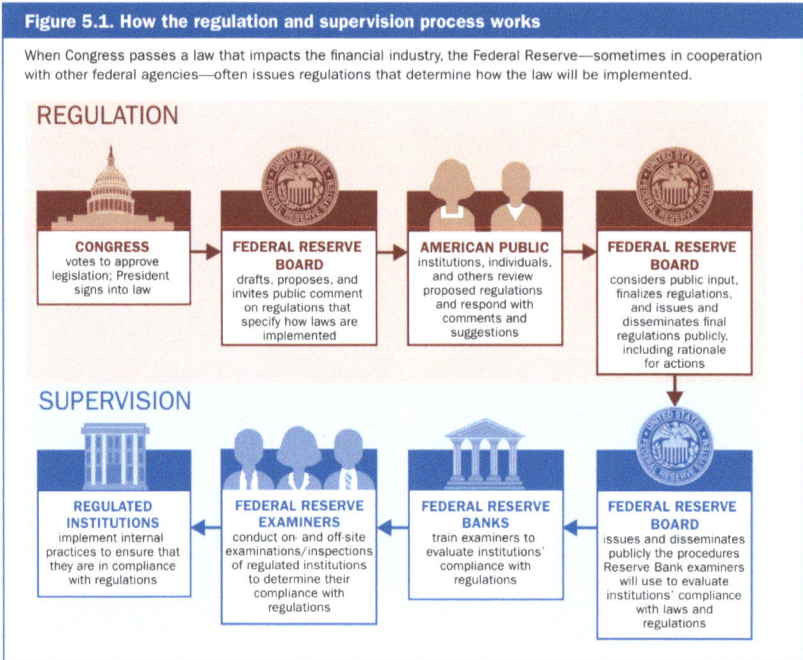

Tier 1: Money creation (public balance sheets) In the U.S. system, most "money" is bank deposits (private IOUs) supported by public infrastructure. The treasury finances appropriated spending by issuing securities. In specific programs, the Federal Reserve may buy Treasuries or agency MBS, affecting the term premiums and bank reserves. The Treasury's account at the Fed, the TGA, is the settlement hub: when the TGA rises, it drains bank Res, and when the TGA decreases, it adds bank Res.

- U.S. Treasury. Issues bills/notes/bonds under statutes; issuance is guided by market demand and debt management policies.
- Federal Reserve. In specific programs, Treasuries/agency MBS may be purchased; these operations affect the term structure and reserves.
- Treasury General Account (TGA). Treasury's Account of the Fed. TGA↑ drains Res; TGA↓ adds Res; large swings can tighten or ease the funding conditions.

34

- Auctions (drainage to TGA). At settlement, investor Dep↓; the investor's bank sends reserves on Fedwire's cash leg; Res↓, TGA↑ (two dashed lines).
- Spending time (added). Outlays debit the TGA and credit the payee bank's Res↑, and the bank then credits the payee's Dep↑ (two solid hops).
- Taxes/fees (drain to TGA). Taxpayer Dep↓; the bank remits Res↓ to TGA (TGA↑) (dashed lines).
- Policy side channel (TGA untouched). Fed buys → Res(Banks)↑, Dep(Non-banks)↑; Fed sells → Res(Banks)↓, Dep(Non-banks)↓.
- Administered rates: IORB (interest on reserve balances) and ON RRP (overnight reverse repo rate) set floors for money market rates; they influence pricing, not the level of Res/Dep level. The ON RRP can absorb cash from the banking system as money funds are balanced at the Fed via tri-party custodians.

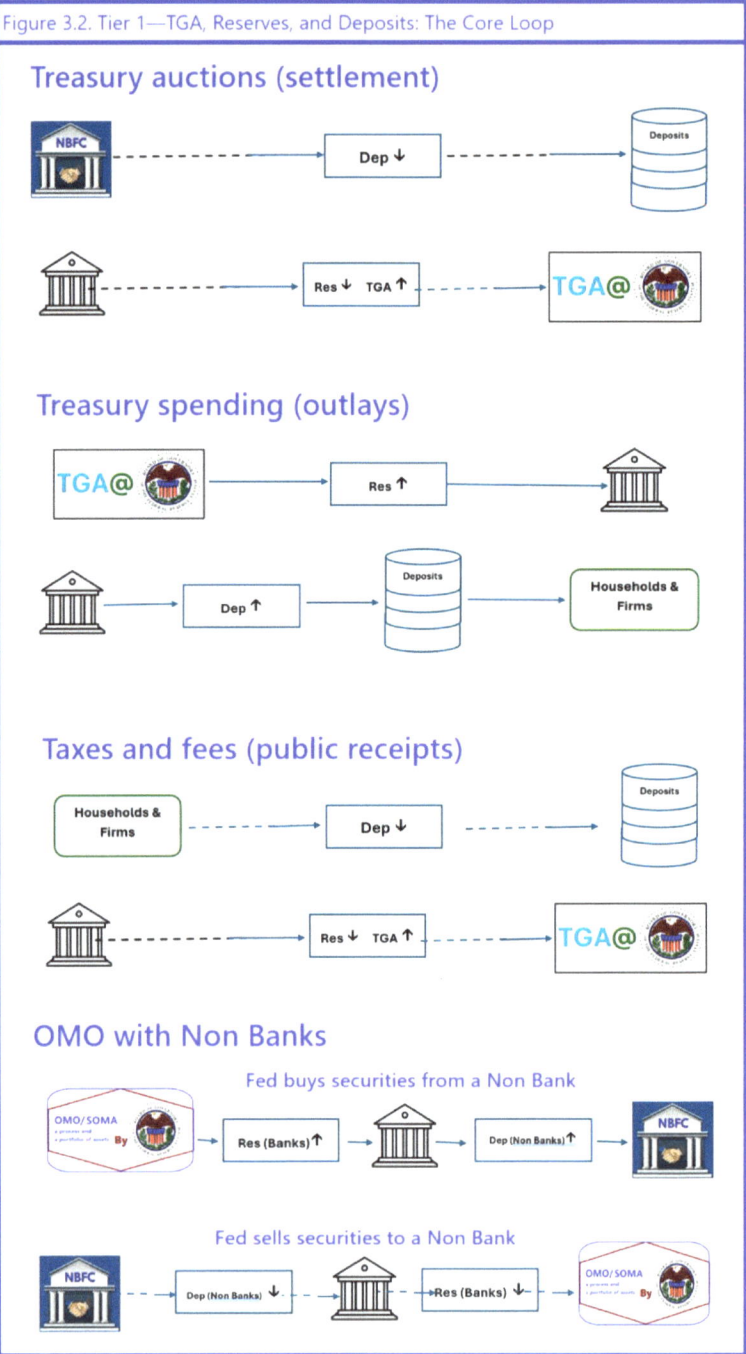

Figure 3.2. Tier 1—TGA, Reserves, and Deposits: The Core Loop

Takeaway. Broad money mostly refers to deposits, and "cash" in circulation is small in comparison. TGA↑ drains, TGA↓ adds Res. When plumbing is tight, stress can quickly appear in the funding markets.

Tier 2: Credit multiplication (banks, markets, and pipes) Banks extend credit within capital and liquidity constraints; non-bank intermediation (repo, money funds, securitization) scales outside the bank balance sheets. When collateral and confidence are strong, credit expands; when funding or haircuts tighten, conditions can reverse. Clearing utilities (e.g., DTCC) underpin large gross flows; systemic risk is chiefly about operational continuity, not gross notional risk.

- Loan origination (creates money). At origination, loan proceeds are credited, Dep↑, and subsequent payments are settled through reserves between banks.
- Repayment. Borrower payments Dep↓; principal is extinguished; interest becomes bank income:
- Sale/securitization. Assets can be sold or securitized, moving loans to investors and reallocating Res/Dep between banks and non-banks; however, the TGA remains unaffected.

Figure 3.3. How the Federal Reserve implements monetary policy

When the Federal Open Market Committee (FOMC) sets monetary policy that, for example, requires lowering the policy interest rate, the Federal Reserve also lowers its administered interest rates. Fed counterparties then make investment decisions by comparing the Fed's administered rates and market interest rates. This comparison causes market rates to decline, which increases borrowing opportunities for households and businesses. These actions allow the FOMC to make progress toward its dual mandate of maximum employment and price stability.

FOMC

FOMC decides to make policy more accommodative ("ease" policy)

OPEN MARKET DESK

The Fed instructs the Desk to reduce the overnight reverse repurchase agreement (ON RRP) offering rate

INTEREST RATES

The Fed reduces its interest on reserve balances (IORB) rate

DESK COUNTERPARTIES

Desk counterparties compare market rates with the Fed's offering rate to decide where to invest their cash

COMPARE RATES

The comparison of the Fed's administered rates with market rates encourages the latter to move down

BANKS

Banks compare market rates with the Fed's IORB rate to decide where to invest their cash

INDIVIDUALS AND BUSINESSES

GROCERIES

With lower rates in the economy, households and businesses see an increased opportunity to borrow for purchases, which influences employment, inflation, and output.

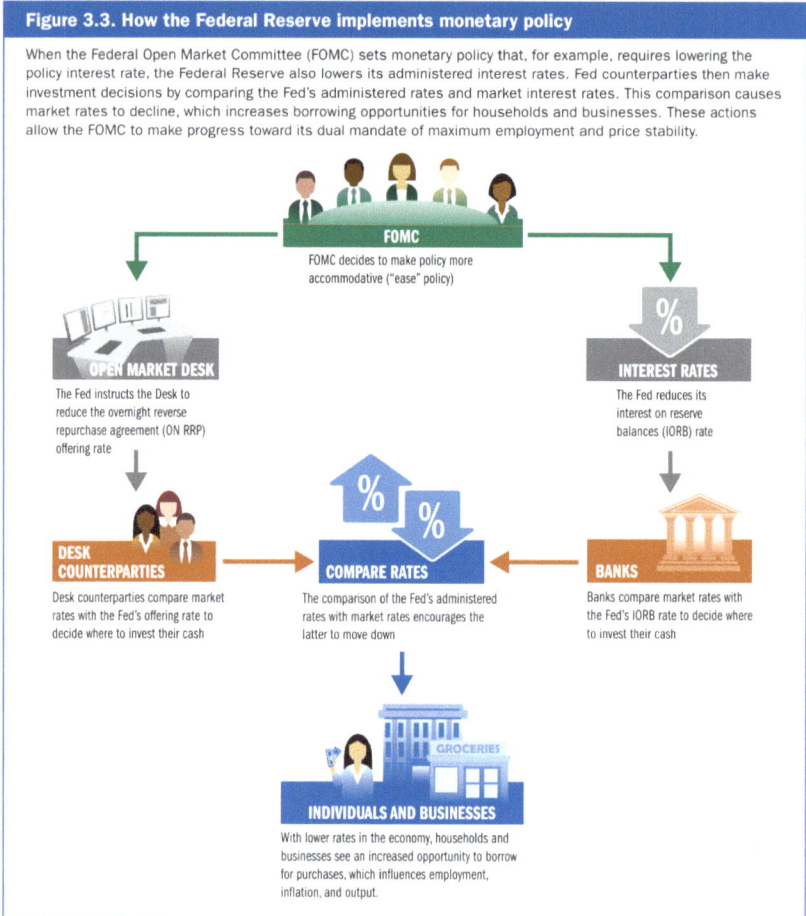

Takeaway. The same structures that scale credit can amplify the tightening.

Tier 3: Real-economy circulation (who actually benefits) Income credits Dep↑ (wages/transfers). Spending moves Dep across banks via ACH/wire/card; velocity depends on turnover, not the deposit level. Corporate payout choices (dividends or buybacks) influence cash settlement. The Federal Reserve Distributional Financial Accounts (DFA) data show a large share of corporate equities held by higher-wealth households, with shares varying by quarter and method.

FedNow improves retail settlement speed, and M2 velocity remains low by historical standards (see M2V).

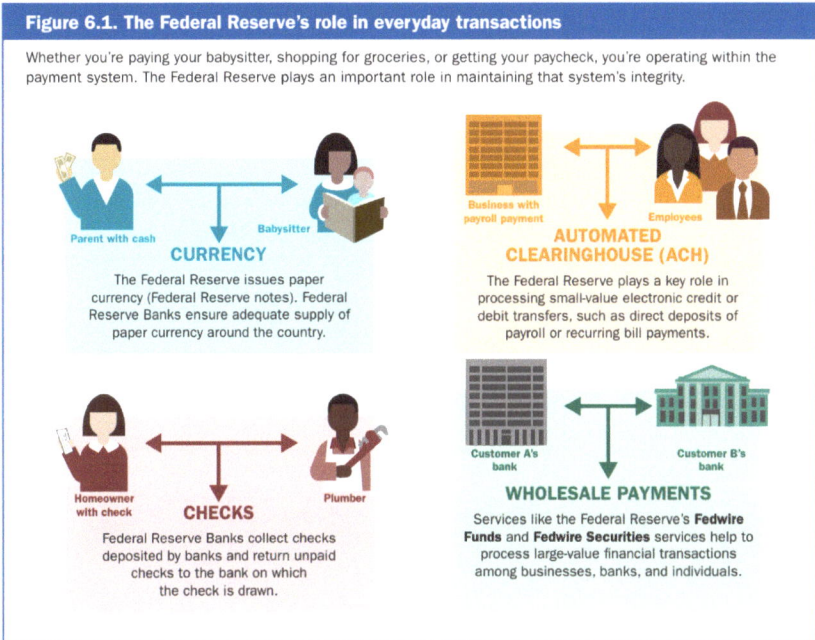

Figure 6.1. The Federal Reserve's role in everyday transactions

Whether you're paying your babysitter, shopping for groceries, or getting your paycheck, you're operating within the payment system. The Federal Reserve plays an important role in maintaining that system's integrity.

CURRENCY
The Federal Reserve issues paper currency (Federal Reserve notes). Federal Reserve Banks ensure adequate supply of paper currency around the country.

AUTOMATED CLEARINGHOUSE (ACH)
The Federal Reserve plays a key role in processing small-value electronic credit or debit transfers, such as direct deposits of payroll or recurring bill payments.

CHECKS
Federal Reserve Banks collect checks deposited by banks and return unpaid checks to the bank on which the check is drawn.

WHOLESALE PAYMENTS
Services like the Federal Reserve's **Fedwire Funds** and **Fedwire Securities** services help to process large-value financial transactions among businesses, banks, and individuals.

Takeaway. Liquidity can recirculate into financial assets rather than into new production; therefore, the distribution of gains depends on the portfolio mix, liability structure, and the cycle.

Tier 4: Drains and external claims As money circulates, interest flows to bondholders, taxes are collected, and part of the income is saved in financial assets. Some outlays flow abroad via foreign holders of U.S. securities. Over time, these drains shape, in which balance sheets accumulate value, and must be adjusted.

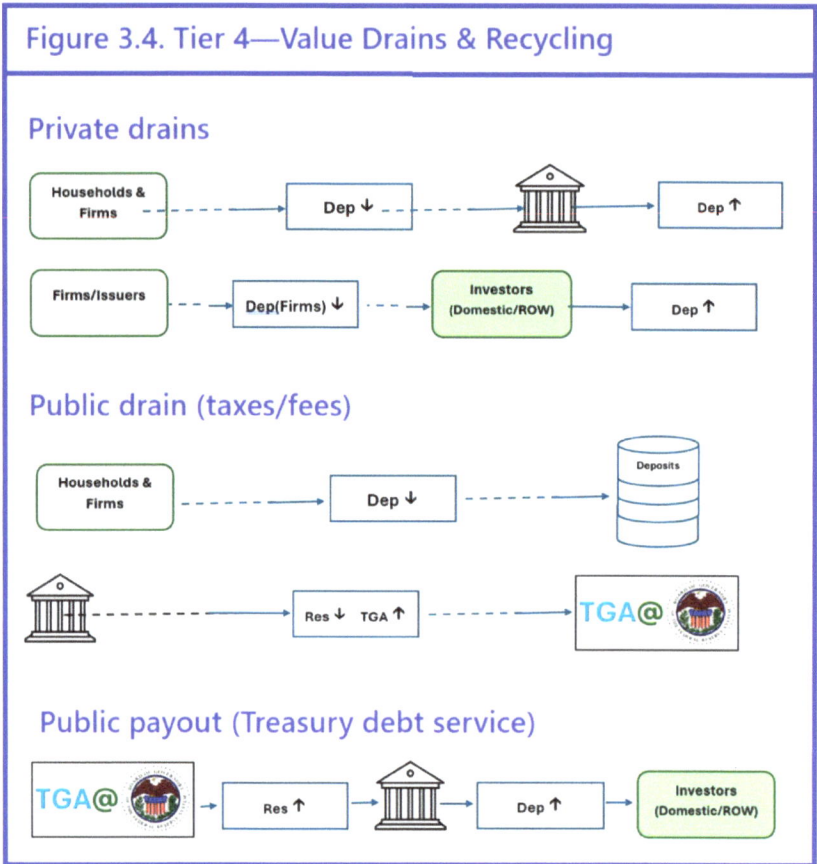

Figure 3.4. Tier 4—Value Drains & Recycling

Takeaway. The system services the senior claims first. Households and smaller firms participate in the remaining activities.

Full System Loop: How It Operates

- Auctions: *Dep↓* (investor), Res↓, TGA↑ (banks→TGA).
- Spending: TGA↓ → Res(Banks)↑ → Dep↑ (payees).
- Credit: origination Dep↑; repayment Dep↓; sales shift Res/Dep across the balance sheets.
- Circulation: income Dep↑; spending Dep shifts via rails.
- Drains: private Dep↓ to banks/investors; public Dep↓; Res↓ → TGA↑; debt service TGA↓ → Res↑ → Dep↑.
- Policy: The Fed buys/sells adjust Res/Dep without touching the TGA.

Fault lines (where stress concentrates)

- Reserve-plumbing sensitivity: Large TGA swings, balance-sheet runoff, or heavy settlements can suddenly tighten funding; the repo/money-fund stress is how it shows.
- Collateral chains and opacity: When haircuts rise or reuse chains shorten, funding can disappear abruptly, and margin calls are transmitted across borders.
- Non-bank leverage outside the bank stress tests: Pensions, insurers, hedge funds, and private credit vehicles can force system-wide responses despite sound banks.
- Run-prone cash pools: Prime money funds and short-term wholesale funding remain vulnerable to rapid outflows in the absence of credible backstops.
- Offshore dollar dependence: Dollar borrowing and offshore lending transmit shocks to domestic systems outside the home country's supervision.
- Concentration in pipes: A small number of CCPs and RTGS systems form operational, single-point failures.
- Household/SME maturity mismatch: Refinancing risk ties outcomes to credit cycles, not just fundamentals.

Insight. When cash is recycled into financial assets faster than wages rise, returns can accrue mainly to existing asset holders, and the outcomes vary by the cycle and portfolio mix.

The Global Layer: A universal financial ecosystem. Architectures repeat across jurisdictions: central bank + Treasury, banks/non-banks, real-time gross settlement (RTGS), and capital markets. Differences appear in scale, openness, and toolkits, and in where stress appears first (FX, collateral haircuts, and clearing bottlenecks).

- Europe (Euro Area and the UK): Eurosystem payment rails (TARGET/T2/TIPS, retail SEPA), bank/covered-bond intermediation, and UK RTGS/CHAPS: The 2022 LDI episode illustrated non-bank leverage/hedging sensitivity.
- Asia (Japan, China, India, and other hubs): BOJ-NET with JGB collateral; CNAPS/CIPS (RMB domestic/cross-border); and).

Regional hubs (Singapore MEPS+ and Hong Kong CHATS) have concentrated on multi-currency settlements.

- Global connectors include SWIFT messaging, CLS PvP FX, Fedwire/CHIPS (USD), TARGET/T2 (EUR), CHAPS (GBP), BOJ-NET (JPY), and CNAPS/CIPS (CNY). Clearing via CCPs (e.g., LCH, CME, JSCC) and central securities depositories (e.g., DTC (DTCC), Euroclear, and Clearstream).

Global Payment & Settlement Rails (Illustrative)

- US: Fedwire/CHIPS for high-value; ACH/instant rails for retail; ON RRP/TGA affects liquidity.
- China: CNAPS for domestic RMB; CIPS provides cross-border RMB clearing.
- India: The UPI enables instant retail transfers, and the RTGS handles high-value gross settlements.
- UK: CHAPS handles high-value same-day sterling payments through the Bank of England.
- EU: TARGET/T2 and SEPA link banks and central infrastructure for euro settlements.

Common pattern. Money and collateral move fast, and stress is transmitted faster through FX swaps, haircut changes, and clearing bottlenecks. Operational risk is concentrated in a small set of CCPs/RTGS rails; continuity matters more than the gross flow size.

The global financial ecosystem is more unified than it appears. Its connective tissue– payment networks, development banks, reserve currency systems, and regulatory forums– ensures that events in one region resonate across the world. For anyone in real estate, banking, or investment, understanding this layer is essential because capital today is inherently international, even when the transaction is local.

Methods and Data. Programs and plumbing (U.S.). Federal Reserve/FRBNY documentation for LSAP/QE (Treasuries, Agency MBS), reserve/TGA mechanics, and September 2019 repo operations. The Figures should refer to the FRED series for TGA (e.g., *WDTGAL/WTREGEN*), Reserve Balances (*WRESBAL/TOTRESNS*), Fed Assets (*WALCL*), ON RRP (*RRPONTSYD*), and M2 velocity (*M2V*). Mortgage rate context from the Freddie MAC

PMMS. Country datasets and institutions differ; methods are portable, but the parameters are localized.

Distribution, payouts, and foreign holders (U.S.). Federal Reserve Distributional Financial Accounts (ownership of equities), S&P Dow Jones Indices (dividends/buybacks), and Treasury TIC (major foreign holders).

Money fund and bank facilities (U.S.). Board press releases/term sheets for the AMLF (2008–10), MMLF (2020), and BTFP (2023–24), plus staff notes/explainers.

Global payments and standards are also included. Eurosystem (TARGET/T2/TIPS, SEPA), BoE (RTGS/CHAPS), BoJ (BOJ-NET), PBOC (CNAPS/CIPS), RBI (RTGS/NEFT/UPI), MAS (MEPS+), HKMA (CHATS), SWIFT, CLS, BIS (banking statistics; Triennial FX Survey), IMF COFER, FSB/IOSCO/BCBS standards.

Replication.
- Pin a date window for every figure/Table (e.g., "2018–2025").
- Where values change frequently (rates, balances), the series is cited, not a single number.
- Post figure scripts, table inputs, and exports are available at www.NestQuestROI.com (Methods and Data).

Endnotes
- FRBNY Liberty Street Economics; Board FEDS Notes ; TGA–Reserves mechanics; September-2019 money-market episode.
- FRED series: WDTGAL/WTREGEN, WRESBAL/TOTRESNS, WALCL, RRPONTSYD, M2V.
- Freddie Mac PMMS (mortgage rates).
- Federal Reserve DFA (equity ownership shares).
- S&P Dow Jones Buyback Quarterly (buybacks/dividends; specify quarter).
- Treasury TIC (major foreign holders; specify month/year).
- DTCC annual disclosures (clearing/settlement volumes; operational continuity notes).
- BIS Quarterly Review (offshore USD liabilities; specify the issue/window).
- M2V: *See Federal Reserve Economic Data (FRED), Velocity of M2 Money Stock (M2V), https://fred.stlouisfed.org/series/M2V; Federal Reserve, FedNow Service advances real-time payments, https://www.federalreserve.gov/newsevents/pressreleases/other20230628a.htm.*

Figure credits
- Fed Figures (1.1, 1.2, 4.1, 5.1, 6.1, 3.3): Source: Author's analysis and redrawn using primary sources ; Board of Governors/FRBNY documentation and FRED series (WDTGAL/WTREGEN, WRESBAL/TOTRESNS, WALCL, RRPONTSYD, M2V).
- Figures (3.1 full loop, 3.2 Tier-1, 3.4 Tier-4): Source: Author's analysis and diagrams (Nest Quest ROI). Legend: Dep = bank deposits; Res = bank reserves; TGA = Treasury General Account. Style: solid = add (↑), dashed = drain (↓).

Chapter 4

Interest-Based Profitability

Definition 4.1: Real Net Interest Margin (RNIM). RNIM = (Loan yield – Cost of funds – Operating cost – Expected loss) – π, where π is the inflation rate over the horizon. RNIM is not a GAAP metric; it is an analytical construct used in this book to compare lending economics in real terms across products and business cycles. It strips out presentation effects (gain-on-sale, hedging, HTM vs. AFS) and asks what spread survives funding, operations, expected loss, and inflation.

Definition 4.2: Equity Return on Asset (ERA). The ERA measures the real return accruing to the equity holder per unit of asset value after inflation. Formally, for period t, ERA_t ≈ ((ΔEquity_t + Cash Distributions_t) / Avg Asset Value_t) – π_t, reported in annual percentage points and deflated by the CPI-U. Worked example (illustrative): If equity increases by $18,000 over a year on an average asset value of $600,000 and CPI-U is 3.0%, then ERA ≈ (18,000/600,000) – 0.03 = 0.03 – 0.03 = 0.00 p.p.; if equity gain is $30,000, ERA ≈ 5.0% – 3.0% = 2.0 p.p. Units: annual percentage points; comparisons deflate cash flows by CPI-U unless otherwise stated.

Example (illustrative). A 30-year fixed-rate mortgage at 6.5% was funded at 4.5%, with an operating cost of 0.7%, expected loss of 0.2%, and CPI of 3.0%: RNIM ≈ (6.5 – 4.5 – 0.7 – 0.2) – 3.0 = –1.9%. If the CPI is 2.0%, the RNIM improves to 0.9%. The point is not the single-year result; it is how thin and condition-dependent the real spread can be.

Units: Annual percentage points; comparisons deflate cash flows by CPI-U unless otherwise stated.

On paper, lending appears stable: it originates a loan, collects interest for decades, and books the spread of the loan. In practice, the spread survives only when funding costs stay contained, loan demand is healthy, credit holds up, and inflation does not dilute long-dated, nominal cash flows. Recent cycles show that funding costs and deposit behavior are moving faster than many plans have assumed, compressing margins even as asset yields rise. (FDIC)

Large U.S. banks illustrate this structure. JPMorgan Chase earned $49.6B in net income in 2023 (record) and ~$54B in 2024, driven by diversified businesses (cards/consumer, markets, assets, and wealth), not by mortgage carry. The Bank of America reported $27.1B in 2024. Diversification cushions firms when a single-product spread thins out; this does not imply that the underlying lending spreads are fat. (Sources: JPMorgan 2023 AR; 2024 earnings materials; Bank of America filings.)

Meanwhile, bank mortgage businesses contracted materially after 2022, as rates reset and gain-on-sale margins tightened. The industry trade press and bank disclosures show lower originations and muted sale margins from 2023 to 2024, with non-bank originators taking shares. (HousingWire, Wells Fargo 4Q23 Earnings)

Why margins compress when conditions shift

Funding costs & deposit betas. As policy rates rose (2022–2024), depositors shifted to higher-yield options (money market funds (MMFs) and treasuries). Banks paid up to retain balances, pushing deposit betas higher and eating into loan spreads, even when loan yields increase. Empirical work and supervisory commentary document a faster pass-through to deposit rates in the current cycle than in the past. (FDIC, Liberty Street Economics)

Liquidity and securities books. Many banks have sizable fixed-income portfolios for liquidity and income generation. Rapid rate increases reduce market values; if hedges are incomplete and deposits move quickly, pressures can become acute, as highlighted by the Federal Reserve's analyses of the Silicon Valley Bank failure. (Federal Reserve)

The industry NIM is cyclical. Aggregate NIM was initially lifted and then moderated as funding costs were caught up, with differing impacts by cohort size. Interpreting reported NIM requires caution: it is nominal, blended, and timing-sensitive. RNIM restores a common real yardstick across cycles and products. (FDIC)

The mechanics behind optics. Different mortgage structures (fixed, ARM, conforming/agency, and FHA/VA) share the same engine: interest income, funding, operation, and loss. The profit presentation varies as follows.

- Originate-to-distribute (gain-on-sale): Upfront revenue depends on secondary market pricing, pipeline hedging, and servicing valuation and is sensitive to rate volatility and bid-ask moves.

- Hold-to-maturity (Carry): Revenue accrues over time and is exposed to funding repricing and inflation risks. In real terms, back-half cash flows contribute less value if the inflation remains high.
- Services (i.e. MSRs): Benefits when prepayments are slow and exposed to valuation swings and hedge costs.

RNIM cuts through presentation: after funding, Opex, expected loss and inflation.

Mortgage reality check (transparent math)
- Present value vs. total interest. Over 30 years at 6.5% monthly compounding (APR), the total nominal interest on a $1,000,000 mortgage is $1,275,444.88. Discounting each month's interest at the loan's monthly rate (i=0.065/12) gives a present interest value of $676,308.44. This gap exists because dollars paid in the future are worth less today. *See Methods 1.1 for discounting conventions and details.*
- RNIM lens. If the all-in cost of funds averages 4.5%, operating cost 0.6–0.9%, expected loss ~0.2–0.3%, and CPI 2–3%, then RNIM ranges from slightly negative to near-zero. Small changes, such as slower prepayment, deposit-mix shifts, or modest CPI upticks, can compress real carries.

This aligns with the 2023–2024 disclosures: lower mortgage volumes and tighter sales margins, even at scale. The appearance of a long and steady revenue stream masks a narrow, condition-sensitive spread. (HousingWire, Wells Fargo 4Q23 Earnings)

Commercial lending: spread on a leash. Commercial loans often float at the policy rates. Rising rates lift nominal yields but also raise borrower debt service, elevate credit risk, and increase banks' funding costs. Portfolio-level spreads that survive provisioning, Opex, and inflation are frequently low. Large banks' earnings underscore the importance of diversification (cards, markets, and wealth) rather than reliance on plain vanilla loan carries. (JPMorgan 4Q24 Earnings Materials)

Implications for modeling (and how Nest Quest ROI uses RNIM)

- RNIM is the right yardstick. Evaluating lending in real terms avoids false comfort from nominal totals and timing effects. Nest Quest ROI applies RNIM to compare across cycles and across products (mortgages, commercials, etc.). (FDIC)
- Condition dependence is a rule of thumb. Funding costs, deposit behavior, and inflation jointly determine whether a loan book earns a real spread or not. The last cycle confirmed that deposit costs could catch up quickly. (FDIC; Liberty Street Economics)
- Presentation ≠ Economics. Gains from sales and servicing can make period earnings appear strong, while long-dated carry remains thin. Disclosures on volumes/margins as a reality check. (HousingWire; Wells Fargo 4Q23 Earnings)
- Fragility is two-sided. Interest burdens borrowers and can be narrow and volatile for lenders, especially when securities books and deposits move in the wrong direction at the wrong time. (Federal Reserve)

Appendix 4.A : Worked mortgage math

- Principal: $1,000,000
- Coupon / Term: 6.5% fixed; 360 months
- Payment: ≈ $6,320.68
- Total nominal interest (lifetime): ≈ $1,275,445
- PV of interest (discounted at 6.5% monthly): ≈ $676,308
- Sensitivity knobs for Nest Quest ROI: prepayment speeds, deposit-beta paths, per-loan Opex, LGD, and CPI scenarios.

Figures are illustrative for pedagogy; the engine is used to generate market-specific outputs.

Appendix 4.B : Accounting views vs. economic RNIM

- Gain-on-sale (originate-to-distribute): Revenue recognized upfront; highly rate- and hedge-sensitive.
- Hold-to-maturity: Interest is recognized over time; the funding mix and inflation drive real economics.

- MSR valuation: Mark-to-model with hedge costs.
- Economic RNIM: Presentation-agnostic real spread after funding, Opex, expected loss and inflation.

Selected sources

- JPMorgan: 2023 Annual Report (record $49.6B net income).
- JPMorgan: 4Q24 earnings materials (full year results).
- Bank of America: 2024 Annual Report/filings (net income $27.1B).
- Mortgage volumes & margins: HousingWire; Wells Fargo ; 4Q23 Earnings.
- FDIC Risk Review and QBP (NIM, deposits/funding): Overview and full report.
- Deposit betas: FDIC/working papers, New York Fed, Liberty Street Economics.
- SVB failure analysis: A Federal Reserve review.

Chapter 5

Persistent Structural Drag

Inflation rarely announces itself with drama; it works quietly through contract escalators, input repricing, vendor renewals, and funding shifts long before nominal statements show stress. Inflation is not an abstract concept for banks. It is a structural drag that narrows spreads, distorts budgets, and converts seemingly solid-interest income into thin or negative real carry.

RNIM lens. From Chapter 4, the real spread is captured by RNIM: interest income minus inflation (cost of funds + operating cost + expected loss). Inflation was not fixed at the time of its origin. It moves with the cycle and keeps repricing the cost side of the P&L (deposits, payroll, technology, audit, and servicing), while the asset side, especially fixed-rate loans, often cannot reprice. When deposit rates and operating costs respond faster than loan yields, the real spread collapses, even if the nominal NIM appears to be stable for some time. Recent cycles have also shown faster pass-through to deposit rates and higher deposit betas *(i.e., the share of policy rate changes passed through to deposit rates)*, pushing up funding costs and squeezing lending spreads. *(Unless noted, CPI refers to CPI-U, and RNIM is expressed in annual percentage points.)* (FDIC, Liberty Street Economics)

Nominal vs. real. Interest income is booked in nominal terms, but funds real expenses: staff, cloud, audit, cybersecurity, and rising deposit costs. A 6.5% coupon on a mortgage or business loan can appear healthy in a spreadsheet. After funding costs, operating expenses (Opex), expected loss, and inflation, RNIM can be near zero or negative, even with perfect borrower performance.

Context (illustrative).
- "Benign-inflation" profile: Loan yield 6.5%; cost of funds 3.5%; Opex 1.0%; expected loss 0.2%; inflation 2.0% → RNIM ≈ −0.2%.

- "Sticky-inflation" profile: Loan yield 6.5%, cost of funds 4.5%, Opex 1.0%, expected loss 0.2%, inflation 3.3% → RNIM ≈ −2.5%.

(Parameters reflect recent CPI ranges and documented deposit pass-through behavior.)

Mortgages vs. business loans (different paths, same results).

- Mortgages (15–30-year fixed). Long durations make them vulnerable to persistent CPI drifts. Even modest average inflation reduces the real value of backloaded cash flows. Real carry depends on whether funding and Opex are kept below the coupon, net of inflation.
- Business loans (shorter, often floating). Nominal yields can move up, but so can borrower costs and banks' funding/OPEX [operating expenditures]. As deposit rates reprice, portfolio-level net interest income can be compressed despite higher asset yields, and dispersion across banks depends on the funding mix and customer behavior. (FDIC, Liberty Street Economics)

The drag propagation.

- Funding: Deposit betas rise; customers shift to higher-yield options (MMFs, Treasuries). Banks pay up, which increases the cost of the funds.
- Operating: Contracts and audits reprice; technology and cybersecurity spending are sticky upward.
- Asset: Fixed-rate loans do not reprice; floating-rate loans can, but borrowers stress and competition cap how far coupons move.
- Reported optics: Firm-level NIM can appear acceptable until the funding/Opex creep is fully demonstrated. RNIM strips optics and measures real economics. (FDIC)

Worked exhibits (transparent and swappable)

Exhibit A: Long-dated mortgage (economic RNIM).

- $1,000,000 at 6.5% (level payment ≈ $6,320.68).
- All-in funding 4.5%; Opex 0.7%; expected loss 0.2%; CPI 3.0% → RNIM ≈ −1.9% (annualized).
- Small shifts in deposit costs or CPI (e.g., +50 bps each) further push the RNIM into the negative territory.

(Method: same amortization as in Chapter 4; swap local parameters to regenerate.)

Exhibit B: Floating-rate commercial loan (economic RNIM).
- $1,000,000 at SOFR + 300 bps (SOFR = Secured Overnight Financing Rate); asset yield 7.0%, cost of funds 4.8%, Opex 1.2%, expected loss 0.3%, CPI 3.3% → RNIM ≈ −2.6%.
- Funding competition +25 bps or Opex +25 bps wipes out the little real spread that remains.

(Purpose: show how deposit pass-through and Opex escalation dominate when inflation persists.)

Insight : Inflation as a systemic drag on lending models
- Interest income is fixed at the origin, whereas inflation is not. The longer the asset duration, the higher the exposure to persistence (not only spikes).
- Costs react faster than coupons. Funding and Opex move with the cycle, whereas fixed asset cash flows do not.
- Diversification masks: They do not erase. Markets/cards/wealth can offset weak real loan carry at the firm level, whereas RNIM rules at the loan-book level. (FDIC)

Implications (for modeling; not prescriptive)
- Evaluate in real terms. Report NIM (nominal), but decide with RNIM (real). Run CPI paths that mirror recent persistence (e.g., 2–3.5%).
- Funding was also provided by the Government. Use high-beta deposit scenarios and competitor MMF/Treasury alternatives; let the cost of funds reprice faster than the asset yields.
- Expose the operating floors. Treat audit, cyber, and cloud as sticky; do not let Opex fall mechanically in a "cooling CPI" case.
- Surface duration risk. For fixed-rate books, RNIM is shown by vintage; for floating-rate books, RNIM is shown under borrower stress constraints (the pricing power is not unlimited).
- Document the measurement choices. Note whether CPI is Dec/Dec vs. annual average; reviewers care about this basis.

NestQuestROI.com

Selected sources

- FDIC: Quarterly Banking Profile (NIM and funding dynamics; cohort dispersion).
- NY Fed: Liberty Street Economics (deposit betas and rate pass-through).
- BLS CPI (recent CPI levels; methodological notes).

Part Two

The Gap Between Earning and Growing

Chapter 6

The Visibility Gap – What Most of Us Don't See

Every household and business operates within a specific context, including income, obligations, risk tolerance, and goals. Some prioritize stability, while others prioritize growth. Some require instant access to funds, whereas others manage long horizons.

However, no universal formula exists for this purpose yet. Most people make high-stakes choices, such as rent versus buy, save versus invest, and borrow versus wait, without a full and structured view of the trade-offs. The system expects action but offers fragments: a loan calculator, a budgeting app, and a retirement projection with idealized assumptions. The issue is not discipline but structured visibility.

Real choices, partial visibility: A modest-income household doing most things "right" still faces recurring uncertainty: buy now or keep renting; how much to save monthly and where to place it; whether $10 a week even matters and what it should fund; and how price volatility complicates plans. Although data exists, they are rarely organized for real-life decisions. Answers matter more than ever, yet they remain elusive.

Tools without understanding the problem: Calculators and applications were also abundant. However, interpretations in this context are scarce. A mortgage calculator returns a payment; it seldom sets that payment in addition to inflation-adjusted taxes, maintenance, or a side-by-side rent comparison using the local dynamics. The result: 'Can I afford the payment?' replaces "Is this sustainable in real terms?" Numbers arrive; strategies do not.

Analytical frame used in this book:
- RNIM (real net interest margin): yield – cost of funds – operating cost – expected loss – inflation.

- Carry timing/idle-days audit: balance × idle days × inflation ÷ 365 = real drag.

(Methods and Data appendix specifies CPI basis, units, and conventions.)

Micro-decisions, macro impact: A small, consistent habit, say $10/week, diverges meaningfully across placements over long horizons. Cash pockets lose ground in real terms when CPI persists; low yields help but may still lag CPI; risk assets or preservation rails add volatility/liquidity trade-offs but can change the long-run profile. The principle holds that small decisions are compounded if guided by clarity. Without such a structure, hesitation is also a compound.

Inflation, budgeting, and fragile planning: A disciplined budget can drift when a few categories are repriced faster than incomes. Ten percent of moves in food or transport over a quarter may seem manageable in isolation; however, shrink buffers, trigger short-term borrowing, or push goals further out. The practical need is to update signals: when to revise the plan, how much, and which assumptions have changed, and so on.

The system was built to move, not to teach. Institutions continuously model risks and opportunities, whereas tools for individuals are often static and fragmented. What is missing is a single pane of glass that (1) projects cash-flow variability at a household's actual income cadence, (2) compares rent vs. buy with inflation-adjusted costs by location, and (3) flags when a plan's real footing no longer holds.

Implications. The modern gap is frequently not income or intent but visibility. Without structured models of how the system moves, people cannot fully utilize it. Part 2 catalogs these gaps. Part 3 introduces testable and system-compatible mechanisms to address these issues.

Sidebar: *An Academic Critique of Grameen Bank Microcredit in Bangladesh.*

> *The Nest Quest ROI platform is dedicated to modeling transparent, collateral-based financial systems that align with globally regulated banking practices. To fully contextualize this approach, it is instructive to examine and critique influential alternative models of financial inclusion, even those based on fundamentally different principles.*

> *The Grameen Bank of Bangladesh, laureled with the Nobel Peace Prize, represents one of the most celebrated examples of micro-credits. However, its group liability lending model has been the subject of significant critical scholarship. A growing body of independent ethnographic and economic research challenges the narrative of unconditional empowerment.*

> *A pivotal work, Lamia Karim's* Microfinance and its Discontents: Women in Debt in Bangladesh *(2011), provides a rigorous analysis of the social dynamics underpinning group lending.[1] Karim's research demonstrates how the mechanism of "social collateral" can be transmuted into a tool of intense peer pressure. This system, which leverages the cultural norms of honor and shame to ensure repayment, often places disproportionate burdens on its primary beneficiaries: women. The result, as documented, can be a cycle of coercion and stress rather than genuine economic liberation, a situation frequently exacerbated by high effective interest rates and mandatory savings schemes that can deepen financial vulnerability.[2, 5]*

> *Further academic critique points to a concerning opacity in the institution's reporting.[3][10] Scholars have argued that the confluence of political influence and donor agendas may have historically obscured a complete and objective understanding of the program's long-term social impact and financial sustainability. This lack of transparent, independent auditing*

makes it difficult to separate empirical results from the promotional narratives.

It is precisely this potential for opacity and social pressure that the Nest Quest ROI's foundational philosophy seeks to avoid. By championing auditable, collateral-based frameworks with clear regulatory oversight, the platform aligns with financial ethics that prioritize transparency and verifiable results. This critical perspective on the Grameen model is not presented to dismiss microfinance entirely but to advocate for the highest standards of accountability and ethical rigor within all financial inclusion efforts.

Nest Quest ROI encourages readers to engage with this critical body of literature. Furthermore, it aligns with academic calls for rigorous, independent, external audits of all microfinance institutions, including the Grameen Bank. Such transparency is the essential first step in validating the model's achievements, addressing its documented shortcomings, and advancing a truly ethical discourse on global financial inclusion.

References

[1](https://www.cadtm.org/The-unfulfilled-promises-of-microcredit-some-new-evidence)

[2](https://journals.uair.arizona.edu/index.php/JPE/article/download/21568/21131)

[3](https://trace.tennessee.edu/cgi/viewcontent.cgi?article=1137&context=pursuit)

[4](https://ssir.org/books/excerpts/entry/microfinance_and_the_backlash)

[5](https://www.tandfonline.com/doi/abs/10.1080/09538251003665446)

[6](https://exhibitions.globalfundforwomen.org/economica/microenterprise/critique-microcredt)

[7](https://studentreview.hks.harvard.edu/the-legacy-of-microfinance-does-it-live-up-to-its-hype/)

[8](https://lirias.kuleuven.be/retrieve/f15628b2-4316-4513-af44-962c8a29add7)

[9](https://www.sciencedirect.com/science/article/abs/pii/S0304387802000871)

[10](https://repository.upenn.edu/bitstreams/b76b17a9-ed21-486a-92e0-a5d9f2e9e4f8/download)

Chapter 7

The Less-Visible Cost of Idle Assets

In institutional finance, capital rarely rests; it rotates, hedges, and compounds. Outside that core, balances often wait for clarity, safety, and the next decision. Idle funds are not neutral; they are active somewhere, but not necessarily for the account holder.

Movement without friction (institutional advantages): Deposits become leverage, idle balances are pooled and lent, and portfolios are rebalanced over time. Institutions transform time into a growth engine. In contrast, most households, small firms, and nonprofits lack the infrastructure to convert waiting periods into disciplined real preservation. This is not a behavioral gap but a structural one.

Idle money is non-neutral. Basic financial identities make the point: real return = nominal return – inflation. When idle balances lag the CPI, purchasing power loses ground even if nominal balances rise. This effect intensifies when interest is nominally taxed. Most people do not receive a clear alert when their money is quietly falling behind.

Two-sided reality of the same deposit: A household reserve of $20,000 earnings at a modest rate may lose ground in real terms during periods of persistent inflation. Meanwhile, the holding institution can recycle that funding into higher-yield activities. One party saves, while the other compounds. This is not misconduct; it is designed to favor those with tools and access.

The visibility gap: Knowing when to act. Private bank clients see portfolio models, inflation scenarios, tax overlays, and risk-adjusted allocations, which are often automated. Most households see a balance and budget. Few receive timely prompts such as, "At current CPI and deposit rates, you are losing ground."

Financial deserts and the excluded majority. Beyond the formally unbanked, many are functionally excluded from compounding due to limited platform access, thin product menus, irregular incomes mismatched to standard tools, or cultural preferences that the system does not integrate. Value then sits in cash pockets, basic wallets, or informal stores; safe in intent but static in effect.

Investment spectrum (illustrative, not advice).
- Public equities: Dividends + capital gains; typical long-run range of approximately 7–10% (period-dependent); high volatility; high liquidity; and medium inflation resilience.
- Broad index funds: Capital gains + dividends, ~7–9%, moderate volatility, high liquidity, and medium inflation resilience
- Government bonds: Interest income; ~2–4%; low volatility; moderate liquidity; and low-inflation resilience.
- Corporate bonds: Interest income, ~3–5%; moderate volatility, moderate liquidity, and low inflation resilience.
- Short-term rentals: Rent + appreciation; ~8–15% (highly operator/market dependent), high volatility, low liquidity, and medium inflation resilience.
- Gold: Price appreciation and long-run purchasing power behavior are discussed in Ch. 8: Low–moderate volatility, high liquidity, and high inflation resilience (period-dependent).
- Crypto assets: Speculative; highly variable returns; extreme volatility; high liquidity; uncertain inflation resilience.
- 401(k)/IRA wrappers: Tax-deferred wrappers (strategy-dependent returns), low liquidity, and medium-inflation resilience.

The ranges are illustrative, sample- and period-dependent, and not forecasts; see Methods and Data for windows, fees, and tax notes for the details.

Implications. Idle capital is rarely a deliberate choice; it grows from visibility gaps, access constraints, and the absence of signals. In the next chapter, we examine a widely trusted anchor that is already used for long-horizon preservation, not as a prescription but as a comparative lens.

Chapter 8

Gold: The Value People Know, The System Overlooks

Policy note (complement, not a challenge). A policy-neutral "anchor rail" can be designed as fiat-in/fiat-out, with standard taxation and reporting, benchmark pricing from established markets, and results evaluated in real terms (e.g., CPI-U). The intent is integration, not replacement. Here, an anchor means a supervised, policy-neutral preservation reference (e.g., gold weight) that complements currency.

Gold is one of the oldest financial assets. Across regions and cultures, it has long served as a store of value and a way to translate purchasing power across time. Many households treat it as practical insurance rather than speculation. This chapter does not "sell" gold; it describes a behavior that the system often does not integrate.

A universal habit is supported by few systems: In many economies, both large and small, households hold gold because it is familiar, divisible, and portable. When formal access is limited or trust is cyclical, people prefer anchors they understand. This is an observed behavior and not a policy statement.

It was practical, not romantic. Gold does not require credit scores, documentation, or specialized knowledge. It does not promise a yield; rather, it aims at retention and purchasing power continuity over multi-year horizons. This does not make it risk-free: prices can be volatile, storage and spread matter, and outcomes depend on the period and fees. The point is descriptive: many savers prefer not to lose rather than to "win big."

What the current rails miss. Institutional rails for custody, benchmarks, and settlements exist, but their integration into daily planning is limited. Most planning tools ignore gold entirely; underwriting models rarely account for supervised small-denomination holdings; and consumer rails seldom offer a simple way to view both currency balances and anchor weights side-by-side.

Preservation vs. speed: Systems tend to reward velocity and margin, whereas anchors reward patience. Bonds can underperform when rates rise, equities can fall, and cash can lose ground under a persistent CPI. A measured role for an anchor with a low correlation to traditional assets can improve planning, even when it does not produce a yield.

Cost of misalignment: Significant household values are located outside the supervised rails in simple, trusted forms. This value is not readily visible in formal planning, underwriting, or community credit. The issue is not the behavior but the design. There is no easy, supervised way to reflect small, regular, and long-term anchor holdings in everyday financial workflow.

Not nostalgia; design: Gold does not require rebranding. It requires integration that is (1) complementary to currency, (2) fully supervised (identity, tax, and prudential standards), (3) transparent about spreads/fees, and (4) usable in small denominations. The objective is not to change the monetary policy but to meet people where they already are.

Implications. Gold is not missing in people's lives; it is missing from mainstream planning rails. Recognizing existing behavior without disrupting policy creates room for tools that preserve the real value between decisions. Part 3 presents implementable supervised models that remain compatible with today's system and are evaluable with the same RNIM lens.

Part Three

Turning Payments Into Equity That Grows Ahead of Inflation and Interest

Chapter 9

The Nest Quest ROI Engine & Simulator

Nest Quest ROI is both an **engine** and a **simulator**. As an engine, it encodes the formal rules that govern cash flow in common structures, traditional rent, mortgages, and other leveraged ownership, rent-to-own (RTO), and hybrid reinvestment models, so identical inputs produce identical, auditable outputs. As a simulator, these rules are exposed to changing conditions such as market trends, taxes and insurance, policy regimes, upkeep and vacancy, and user-chosen reinvestment; thus, outcomes can be studied rather than assumed. The purpose is straightforward: to transform beliefs about finance into statements that can be tested against ledgers.

The methodological framework is simple and reproducible. First, the assumptions are defined. Second, model-specific flows are applied: a mortgage amortizes interest and principal; pure rent treats payment as consumption; and RTO divides payment transparently across consumption, equity credit, and shared operating costs, with ownership shares updating mechanically over time. Third, the system advances periodically, booking appreciation, upkeep, vacancy, fees, and reinvestment according to the same calendar across models. Finally, the simulator reports and compares results in both nominal and CPI-adjusted (real) terms, so general price drift cannot be mistaken for a genuine gain. In short, each model faces the same weather; differences arise from the design, not from uneven treatment.

The benchmark set includes traditional rent (tenant and owner views), mortgage/leveraged ownership, RTO, and hybrids such as RTO + Digital Gold Savings Account (DGSA) and RTO + Stock. RTO serves as the organizing spine because it converts a recurring expense into a measurable path to ownership while making responsibilities and exit mechanics, explicit. The DGSA serves as a preservation rail: deposits and withdrawals are in fiat; balances are shown in grams and local currency;

and custody and disclosures adhere to existing rules, complementing, not challenging, monetary policy.

To make the chapter easy to use in practice, the elements that you tune and the artifacts you receive are enumerated below; everything else remains in a flowing prose.

Inputs & Parameters

- Invested amount in asset: Starting capital committed; defines initial exposure, and capacity to absorb shocks.
- Investment term (horizon): Total run length; small changes compound into large differences in the results.
- Asset appreciation rate: Expected property value growth, a major driver of real estate returns in any model.
- Rent growth rate: The expected rent change over time affects both affordability and the owner's yield.
- Property tax rate: Jurisdiction-specific annual levy that converts the headline yield into net reality.
- Insurance rate: Long-horizon cost that often rises stepwise and must be booked as an operating friction.
- Maintenance cost: Required upkeep as a share of value or rent; underinvestment reduces durability and resale value.
- Vacancy rate: Expected time off-market; even short episodes materially affect realized returns.
- Rental administration fee: Screening, advertising, and management costs, necessary if not self-managing.
- Loan interest rate (and schedule): Cost and timing of debt service for mortgage runs shape cash flow stress.
- RTO rent portion (consumption): The fraction of payment is treated as use and anchor affordability.
- RTO equity build portion: The fraction credited to ownership that defines the pace of share accumulation.
- Standard rent factor (1/180 heuristic): Orientation linking asset value to monthly rent; a starting point, not a rule. We treat 1/180 as an orientation only and calibrate it to local rent/value distributions

using recent comparables; the engine adjusts the anchor to the observed medians/quantiles.

- DGSA starting gold price: Baseline for preservation rail; used to mark conversions and balances.
- DGSA appreciation assumption: Long-run gold returns are used for scenario comparison, not for prediction.
- Reinvestment split: Cadence and share of surplus directed to the DGSA and/or other assets.
- Stock growth rate (benchmark): Reference track for equity markets to enable a fair comparison with the hybrids.
- Monthly contribution (optional): Steady additions that test the scaling of small and disciplined inputs.
- Exit timing and sell cost: Year of disposition plus brokers' fees and transfer costs; the final arbiter of the realized proceeds.

Outputs & Reports
- Full cash-flow ledgers: Period-by-period inflows/outflows for each leg (consumption, equity, costs, reinvestment, and debt service if applicable). Exports include the ruleset version, parameter hash, CPI series ID, discount convention, and day-count basis (replicable).
- Equity path and ownership share: Evolving shares over time; critical for the RTO analysis.
- DGSA specifics: Reinvested capital, grams accumulated from equity payouts, and gold value at the exit.
- Exit statement: Exit value = cashflow + equity + appreciation – sell cost; net sale proceeds after costs/obligations.
- Performance metrics: ROI, IRR, Cash-on-Cash Return, with an optional CPI-adjusted (real) view.
- Comparative dashboards: Like-for-like summaries placing models on the same axes and time lines.

Outcomes & Findings
- Profitable-looking debt can lag in real terms: Thin spreads paired with rising operating costs compress real performance even when loans "perform."

- Rent is not destiny: Transparent allocation can convert a share of payments into ownership without hiding friction or overstating the yield.
- Friction is first-order: Taxes, insurance, maintenance, vacancies, and exit fees often determine outcomes more than headline appreciation.
- Idle cash is never neutral: An unallocated surplus benefits someone, just not the depositor, and rule-based reinvestment changes the long-run picture.
- Timing flips leaderboards: Small differences in horizon, exit year, or reinvestment cadence can reverse the model that dominates.

These observations are not opinions; they fall directly out of the arithmetic once all flows are placed on the same time line.

Governance and Neutrality: The engine favors governed models over narratives. The allocation rules are explicit and identical across the runs. The DGSA is policy-neutral; fiat in, fiat out, with balances viewable in grams and currency, and custody and disclosure are handled under existing rules. RTO contracts specify hardship treatment, upkeep standards, and exit settlement in advance to avoid ambiguity at the worst moment. For reviewers and partners, audit-ready exports allow any claims to be recomputed independently.

How Readers Use the Engine. Nest Quest ROI provides everyone with the same transparent ledger and engine. Households compare rent, mortgage, and rent-to-own, see lifetime cost, equity pace, and exit math before committing; students and educators run a reproducible lab; lenders and investors design and stress-test products under identical assumptions and share parameter blocks for verification; real estate operators test hold-renovate-reposition choices against measured cash flows; and policymakers trace how taxes and rules move through balance sheets in nominal and inflation-adjusted terms. One method, one engine: See the evidence, choose the trade-offs and rerun them with your numbers.

Defined Terms - Consumption leg; equity credit (and equity-credit rate); operating-cost ledger; hardship reversion; exit waterfall; pricing anchor; gram ledger; valuation layer; buffer SLA; attestation.

Implications. This chapter establishes the engine's role and discipline: the same inputs, the same weather, and fair comparisons. Chapter 10 examines Rent-to-Own (RTO) as a transparent allocation contract that turns a portion of the payment into measurable ownership with symmetric responsibilities and fair-exit mechanics. Chapter 11 presents the Digital Gold Savings Account (DGSA) as an auditable preservation rail that coexists with sovereign currency and strengthens planning between opportunities. Chapter 12 evaluates RTO + Gold against peers such as RTO + Stock, showing when and why the combination delivers a balanced mix of growth and stability. The engine does not ask for belief; it invites inspection and leaves the choice to the reader.

Chapter 10
Rent-to-Own: A Transparent Pathway to Shared Ownership

Rent-to-own (RTO) is a contract architecture that converts a necessary expense, housing use, into a measured path to ownership without inheriting the brittleness of fixed-debt schedules. It maintains the immediate utility of renting, adds disciplined equity credit, and allocates operating burdens in proportion to the evolving ownership shares. Because the allocation rule is transparent and the ledger is auditable, trust rests on design rather than hope alone.

Positioning. Renting maximizes flexibility but never transfers titles. Mortgages transfer title but lock households into rigid amortization, which can clash with shocks to income, taxes, insurance or policies. RTO occupies the middle ground: it preserves use, grows ownership continuously, shares burdens symmetrically, and specifies hardship and exit terms before payment is made. This combination of use, accruals, symmetry, and governance produces a contract that families can understand, institutions can underwrite, and policymakers can evaluate.

Mechanics in Motion. Each payment is posted to three subledgers: the consumption leg compensates for housing services and never converts them into ownership. The equity credit leg increases the resident's ownership share from that date forward, so appreciation (and, if applicable, depreciation) is shared pro rata and in real time. Operating costs, such as taxes, insurance, and maintenance, are booked by share; as the residents' share rises, so do their responsibilities. Hardship is handled by reversion: for a defined period, payments can temporarily shift to consumption plus proportional operating costs, pausing equity credit without erasing the equity already earned. Exit is a settlement, not a cliff: consumption remains consumption; equity, together with the resident's share of net appreciation, is reconciled against a current, independent valuation and a pre-agreed Exit Waterfall.

RTO-Specific Inputs & Parameters

- Starting ownership share. Initial resident and sponsor stakes (including any down payment or contribution in kind) set the baseline for responsibility and participation in value changes.
- Consumption vs. equity splits. The contract fraction of each payment priced as use versus credited to ownership determines the affordability and the slope of the ownership path.
- Operating cost allocation rule. The proportional booking of taxes, insurance, and maintenance by the current share may include thresholds where neglected upkeep delays equity credit until it is remedied.
- Hardship Reversion Terms. Triggers (income shocks and medical emergencies), maximum duration, cure mechanics, and automatic resumption preserve continuity without windfalls.
- Capital improvement policy. The approval process, cost-sharing, and how improvements adjust shares or are reimbursed at the exit prevent opportunistic upgrades or neglecting.
- Appraisal and exit protocols. Valuation standards (e.g., independent averaged appraisals), frequency, and broker/closing-cost allocation ensure settlement integrity.
- Pricing anchor. A localized rent–value orientation (e.g., the 1/180 heuristic as a starting point) with documented local variance avoids speculative over- or under-pricing.
- Late-payment handling. Grace windows, non-punitive fees aligned with cost recovery (not equity forfeiture), and the sequence of hardship triggers.
- Background leverage (if any). Whether the sponsor finances the asset in the background and how the risk is insulated from the resident's performance keeps the household's obligations clean.
- Jurisdictional guardrails: Consumer disclosures, fair housing and tenancy rules, and escrow practices suitable to the venue; the contract is implemented within the existing law.

RTO-Specific Outputs & Reports

- Ownership-share trajectory. The resident's share over time, with key waypoints (25%, 50%, 75%) and the calendar dates at which they are crossed under the current performance.
- Equity-credit rate. The pace at which equity credits translate into shares, net of any upkeep gating, highlights how maintenance discipline affects ownership.
- Use cost versus equity delta. The portion of payment that is pure consumption relative to equity credit and operating burdens; that is, the "effective cost of living" alongside "effective capital formation."
- Operating-cost ledger. Periodized attribution of taxes, insurance, and maintenance by share, including any deferred maintenance holds and later releases.
- Hardship Reversion Diary. The start/end dates of any reversion, payments made during the reversion, and automatic resumption outcomes demonstrate cash flow continuity without equity destruction.
- Exit Waterfall. Sale price, costs, and precise distribution: consumption retained by the sponsor, residents' equity returned, sponsor's share returned, and appreciation/depreciation allocated by the final shares.
- Comparative placement. The RTO ledger is presented adjacent to the rent and mortgage ledgers under the same city-level costs and horizon, so the differences are attributable to contract design, not to mismatched assumptions.

What RTO Changes and Why It Works? The RTO aligns incentives in such a way that rent and mortgages do not. As the resident's share grows, so do both rights and responsibilities; the sponsor's return depends not only on the time value but also on the asset's actual performance, shifting the relationship from creditor–debtor to co-owners with defined roles. This alignment improves resilience: Hardship Reversion keeps payments flowing and families housed while protecting already-accrued equity; sponsors avoid vacancy and legal friction; and exits are governed by protocol rather than panic. Because operating frictions are explicit and priced by shares, the model rewards upkeep and penalizes neglect in a predictable, non-punitive way. As contract prices are used separately from ownership, they expose the true cost of living alongside the true pace of wealth formation, a clarity missing from both rent and mortgage narratives.

A compact scenario. A household localizes the pricing anchor to its neighborhood, sets a modest equity-credit fraction to keep payments manageable, and agrees with maintenance thresholds that gate further equity if they are neglected. After an income shock in year three, the contract reverts for four months to consumption plus costs only; equity pauses but is not lost to residents. In year ten, with the resident at 42% ownership, both parties opt to sell; the Exit Waterfall returns the resident's equity plus 42% of net appreciation and returns the sponsor's share plus retained consumption and 58% of net appreciation. Placed next to the rent and mortgage ledgers for the same horizon, the differences are not rhetorical; the numbers show the trade-offs plainly.

Governance Principles. Hardship and cure are defined ex ante, equity credit can be conditioned on documented upkeep, appraisals follow a neutral standard with cost allocation fixed in advance, make-whole schedules deter opportunistic exits while keeping settlements fair, and change control prevents mid-contract surprises. The goal is not to predict the future but to narrow the path of acceptable behavior so that both sides can plan.

Implications. The RTO is a payment-allocation contract that turns housing use into transparent co-ownership, balancing flexibility with discipline. It reduces the fragility of foreclosure dynamics, rewards maintenance, and converts "rent forever" into a credible path to the title without importing the full rigidity of debt. However, equity alone does not guarantee preserved purchasing power. The next chapter introduces the Digital Gold Savings Account (DGSA), a policy-neutral preservation rail that stabilizes value between opportunities and completes the arc from use to ownership to enduring worth.

Chapter 11
The Digital Gold Savings Account (DGSA)

Liquidity is essential; however, unanchored cash steadily loses purchasing power through inflation, policy shifts, and monetary expansion. The Digital Gold Savings Account (DGSA) pairs the convenience of digital banking with a savings anchor that has preserved its value across centuries. In contemporary finance, most wealth already exists as digits; the decisive difference is what these digits represent. Bank cash is a claim within a policy-managed system, and a DGSA balance is a claim on gold weight, which is always recorded and redeemed in the local currency. One floats with policy, while the other references a globally recognized store of value. The point is not to challenge the monetary order but to give households and institutions a policy-neutral place to hold savings between opportunities.

A DGSA is a savings account that shows two simultaneous balances: local currency and gold grams. Deposits and withdrawals occur in the local currency that you already use, and grams are the reference measure that anchors the long-term purchasing power. If an account holder deposits $240 when gold is $100/gram, the account immediately shows $240 and 2.4 g. The balance remains liquid in currency terms, but the saver can see and track its underlying weight. This dual display transforms abstract inflation hedges into everyday ledgers.

The DGSA operates within the existing financial architecture. Providers apply customer protection and prudential standards, deliver consumer disclosures on price volatility and fees, maintain fiat liquidity pools for redemptions, and arrange independent reserve attestations. Under ordinary rules, balances remain taxable and reportable. Central banks retain full control of monetary tools, governments collect taxes in the national currency, and banks offer DGSA alongside other savings products. In practical terms, the DGSA sits with money markets and brokerage sweep accounts as a functional reinforcement, not a structural replacement.

Operating Mode: Deposits arrive in the local currency and are converted into grams at a published policy, sourced either from allocated reserves or market purchases. The balances display both currencies and grams in real time. Redemptions are paid out in the local currency at the prevailing conversion rate, supported by layered liquidity buffers sized according to expected flows. Providers earn modest conversion spreads and transparent fees, similar to FX or securities settlements. Fractional-gram accounting makes the product accessible to small savers, and security, custody, and reporting match bank-grade expectations.

Why Do Households, Banks, and Systems Benefit? For households, the DGSA offers a stable savings rail without forcing exposure to instruments that they do not have time to monitor. Banks deepen depositor trust and add fee-generating services that perform well during inflationary stress. For policymakers, the DGSA reduces fragility by allowing the public to hold value in a form that does not depend on perfectly stable prices, thus dampening the pressure for ad-hoc interventions. In regions where households already trust gold, the DGSA formalizes the existing behavior and routes it through supervised institutions.

KYC/AML and Customer Due Diligence. The DGSA uses the same identity, screening, and monitoring disciplines that banks apply to deposit and custody products. The objective is simple: to keep the rail system safe, lawful, and interoperable with the broader system.
- Identity verification and residency checks: Government-issued ID verification, residency confirmation, and, where relevant, beneficial owner declarations for businesses.
- Sanctions, PEP, and adverse media screening: Automated checks at onboarding and on a rolling basis; enhanced due diligence (EDD) when risk indicators are present.
- Source of funds/source of wealth review: Proportional to risk; documentary evidence requested where profiles warrant.
- Ongoing monitoring: Rule-based and behavior-based surveillance with suspicious activity reports filed as required by law.

- Threshold reporting and record-keeping: Jurisdiction-specific reporting of large cash transactions/transfers with retention schedules aligned with statutes.
- Risk-based refresh: Periodic KYC renewal keyed to the risk tier, material profile changes, or trigger events (e.g., unusual conversion activity).
- Data security: Strong authentication (e.g., MFA), encryption at rest/in transit, hardware security modules for key materials, and independent penetration testing are required.

These controls keep the DGSA firmly inside the regulated perimeter: funds enter and exit on ordinary bank rails, customers are known, activities are monitored, and audit trails are preserved.

Taxation & Reporting. The DGSA does not introduce an exotic tax treatment; it maps to familiar categories already used for bank savings and financial assets. The core ideas are the tax base, timing, and jurisdiction.

Deposits and withdrawals in local currencies are not taxable events. Moving money from a checking account to a DGSA (or vice versa) does not create income per se. A bank deposit is not a purchase of a good or service; therefore, a sales tax/VAT does not apply to the deposited money. (Separate point: some jurisdictions levy VAT/sales tax on retail bullion purchases.) Many exempt "monetary gold." How DGSA conversions are treated depends on the local law and the product's legal form. Providers disclose this clearly.)

Gains and losses are generally taxed on realization, not on daily repricing. In most jurisdictions, merely holding a position that fluctuates in value does not trigger tax. A taxable gain (or deductible loss) typically occurs when grams are converted back to currency or are otherwise disposed. The cost basis is the currency value of the grams when acquired; the realized gain/loss equals the redemption proceeds minus the cost basis (net of fees).

- If the jurisdiction treats gold like other capital assets, gains are taxed under capital-gains rules, and losses may offset other gains (subject to limits).
- If gold is treated as a collectible or commodity, a different rate schedule may apply.
- A minority of jurisdictions impose mark-to-market or wealth taxation; in these cases, periodic valuation may be required even without redemption.

No "double taxation": different taxes apply to different bases.
Income or capital-gains tax applies to economic gain (the appreciation realized when grams are redeemed to currency or when income is distributed; the DGSA has no "interest," so the usual case is capital gain on redemption).

- Sales tax/VAT; where it applies to bullion, targets the consumption of goods, not the act of holding money or saving. Many regimes entirely exempt monetary gold from VAT, while others exempt it above certain purity thresholds or in a wholesale form.
- Bank fees/spreads are not taxes; they are disclosed costs that reduce net gains, as brokerage fees do for the securities.

The reporting followed familiar patterns. Providers issue year-end statements summarizing conversions, redemptions, and cost basis movements so that customers can compute realized gains/losses. Where required, providers also file information returns with the tax authorities. If the account pays promotional rewards or cash incentives, it may be reported as an ordinary income under local rules.

Practical bottom line.
- If there is a realized gain (you redeemed grams for more than your cost basis), expect tax on the gain according to the local rule.
- If there is a realized loss, you may receive loss treatment or credits/offsets, subject to the jurisdictional limits of your country.
- If you hold the entire period without redemption and your jurisdiction does not impose a mark-to-market or wealth tax, there is

typically no tax for that period, just as with unrealized gains in many brokerage accounts.

Because tax regimes differ, institutions provide clear tax guides, and customers should confirm treatment with a qualified advisor in their jurisdiction.

Note: This chapter describes general mechanisms and not tax or financial advice, as the treatment varies by jurisdiction. Readers should consult with qualified advisors for further information.

Addressing Common Questions

Ownership & custody. Customers own gold claims represented by the weights displayed in their accounts. Providers document whether custody is allocated (specific bars/coins attributed) or pooled (fungible weight under the trust). In either case, the claim is independent of the provider's corporate assets.

Liquidity and stress. As with deposits, providers plan for withdrawals: fiat pools first, reserves, and then market execution. Stress procedures and temporary gates are disclosed upfront, which is rare when the buffers are prudently sized.

Pricing & market data. The DGSA references public gold markets. Providers publish their sourcing, feed aggregation, and cutoff rules. No single institution "sets" the gold prices.

Regulatory stance. The DGSA uses local currency rails, complies with the KYC/AML, and reports taxes. It does not bypass the regulation; it operates within it, similar to other custody or savings products.

Banks' incentives. Banks do not lose relevance; they gain a trusted savings product that attracts deposits, generates conversions, and lengthens relationships, which are especially valuable during inflationary cycles.

Scale and small savers. Fractional-gram accounting makes DGSA granular. A few dollars a week accumulate into weight; visibility is the point.

FX and USD quoting. Gold is often quoted in USD, but balances are always shown in grams and local currency. Redemptions are settled in local currency at transparent rates.

Security and provider failure. The DGSA requires bank-grade controls and clear legal segregation. If a provider fails, customers' gold claims remain enforceable against segregated pools of assets.

Ethics and environmental considerations. Most demand can be met from above-ground stocks; when new sourcing is used, providers can adopt certified responsible supply chains.

Misuse & compliance. Integration with supervised banks, mandatory KYC/AML, and transparent pricing maintains the DGSA within legitimate finance. However, this product is unsuitable for off-grid use.

Horizon & mis-selling. The DGSA is a savings rail, not a day-trading venue. Disclosures emphasize long-term preservation, whereas price paths can fluctuate in the short term.

Macro neutrality. The DGSA neither pegs the currency to gold nor limits the policy capacity. It simply offers households a way to save weight while transacting currency.

Crowding-out investment. Savings and investment are complementary. The DGSA preserves the savings slice; households and institutions still invest in businesses, real estate, and markets with the investment slice.

Adoption curve. New products gradually diffuse into the environment. The combination of dual-balance visibility and lived experience tends to build trust over time, exactly how online banking and retirement accounts have become the norm.

A Short Illustration. A household decides to move any surplus above its emergency threshold into the DGSA on each pay day. Over a year, they convert small amounts into fractional grams; their cash accounts remain ready for bills and contingencies, while their DGSA shows a growing weight and currency value at the current prices. In year three, they redeem a portion to fund a planned expense; the provider's statement shows the cost basis, proceeds, and realized gain for tax reporting. Over five years, the weight acts as a purchasing power anchor, which is not perfectly smooth but more resilient than idle cash. Operationally, it behaves like a savings account. Conceptually, it stores value in weight.

Implications. The DGSA does not change how money is issued, taxed, or spent; however, it changes how savings behave between opportunities.

By anchoring part of the household and institutional balances to weight rather than policy expectations, the DGSA reduces fragility without constraining policies or commerce. For banks, it is a compliant product line; for governments, an ally in resilience; and for families, a way to make time work for savings instead of against them.

The next chapter integrates these pieces. RTO builds ownership through transparent payment allocations. The DGSA preserves purchasing power between opportunities. RTO + DGSA; growth plus preservation; turns a household's or institution's financial path into a governed cycle rather than a gamble.

Chapter 12

RTO + Gold: The Model of Growth and Preservation

Two rails, one method: it unites the two forces that modern finance has long struggled to reconcile: the need for steady, reliable growth and the need to safeguard wealth against inflation.

The Rent-to-Own structure generates consistent cash flows from investments while allowing households to transition from renters to owners. These flows are secured by equity rather than interest, aligning incentives, or embedding safeguards. Even in the presence of risk, struggling borrowers, and RTO contracts are designed with structured exit strategies and shared control of assets, ensuring that institutions are protected and participants retain a fair path forward.

The Digital Gold Savings Account amplifies this structure by ensuring that every payment received can be reinvested under disclosed conversion policies and standard settlement windows. Unlike traditional lending, which requires continual borrower acquisition, risk management, and marketing, the DGSA anchors surplus flows in a store of value that is intended to preserve purchasing power across many regimes (outcomes remain horizon- and cost-dependent).

Together, the result is dual reinforcement: equity accumulation on one side and inflation-resilient preservation on the other. Investors gain governed cash flow with compounding effects from reinvested surpluses, institutions gain efficiency and trust, and households build enduring wealth. It is not growth at the cost of stability or preservation without expansion; it is both, seamlessly integrated.

RTO + Gold offers a mathematically sound, operationally efficient, and universally adaptable framework that demonstrates how finance can align profitability with stability and create benefits for households, institutions, and governments.

Institutional and Systemic Benefits. The appeal of RTO + Gold extends beyond the household. For financial institutions, the model creates a steady cash flow and provides a transparent reinvestment channel. Instead of continually bearing the costs of borrower acquisition and credit management, institutions can rely on RTO agreements to generate predictable inflows while simultaneously strengthening their reserves through the DGSA. This dual structure builds profitability while enhancing the resilience of institutions.

For investors, attraction lies in their efficiency and predictability. Rent-to-own produces contractual equity transfers, whereas the DGSA automatically preserves the surplus funds in a trusted global asset. This combination eliminates idle balances, produces compounding effects from reinvested surpluses, and allows wealth to accumulate and be safeguarded without dependence on speculative cycles.

This model contributes to the systemic stability of the government and policymakers. By anchoring wealth in ownership and gold, households are less vulnerable to inflation shocks and debt traps, lowering their need for costly emergency interventions. The financial system gains stability by complementing these mechanisms that reinforce household confidence rather than replacing sovereign currencies or monetary policies.

Global and Cultural Relevance: The strength of RTO + Gold lies not only in its mechanics but also in its wide recognition. Gold is trusted worldwide as a store of value, and property ownership remains a universal marker of security and stability in the country. By combining these two anchors, Nest Quest ROI creates a model that is globally adaptable, culturally familiar and structurally innovative.

This adaptability ensures that RTO + Gold is not confined to any specific geographical or economic systems. It can be integrated into advanced economies seeking inflation protection, emerging markets working toward financial inclusion, and regions where gold and property serve as symbols of stability. In every context, the logic remains consistent: growth and preservation are aligned, rather than opposed.

Comparison of RTO + Gold with Other Reinvestment Models. The Nest Quest ROI framework is designed to provide investors and institutions with a transparent platform for evaluating multiple, reinvestment strategies. While the RTO + Gold model offers a reliable safeguard under many regimes (as modeled), subject to horizon, costs, and local market conditions, other reinvestment options may be attractive depending on investors' goals, risk appetite, and institutional strategy. The Nest Quest ROI does not prescribe a single path; it enables a clear comparison so that choices are informed by evidence rather than assumptions.

RTO + Stock. Pairing Rent-to-Own cash flows with stock market reinvestment can generate significant returns during periods of equity expansion. For investors prioritizing higher growth potential and being comfortable with market volatility, this model offers a legitimate alternative. However, stocks remain sensitive to speculation, economic cycles, and systemic shocks, which means that outcomes can vary widely across time horizons. Within Nest Quest ROI, investors can model these dynamics and assess whether the potential growth of equities outweighs the associated risks compared to gold or real estate reinvestment.

RTO + Real Estate. Surpluses generated from RTO agreements can also be directed toward additional property ventures. This approach builds on the same ownership logic as the RTO and can accelerate portfolio expansion. Simultaneously, it introduces concentration risks, higher management costs, and sensitivity to local regulations, taxes, and market conditions. For some institutions, expanding real estate holdings aligns with their strategy, while for others, the liquidity and universality of gold or equities may be more preferable. Nest Quest ROI simulations provide a structured means of comparing these outcomes, helping decision-makers understand the trade-offs between long-term stability and concentrated growth.

When RTO + Gold can underperform

- Prolonged flat/negative real property performance combined with high operating friction.
- Gold price stagnation over a specific horizon or elevated spreads/fees.
- Exit-year slippage (selling in a weak year) and maintenance overruns that exceed the assumptions.

Investor Choice and Flexibility. Not all investors seek the same outcome. Some may prioritize the stability and inflation resilience of gold, while others may pursue the higher but more variable returns of equities or the tangible expansion of real estate. In the absence of a DGSA, reinvestment may take the form of physical gold or other traditional asset purchases. What distinguishes the Nest Quest ROI is that it allows all these options to be modeled side by side, using the same assumptions and transparent metrics. This enables households, institutions, and policymakers to align strategies with their specific goals, whether they emphasize preservation, growth, or expansion.

Implications. Nest Quest ROI does not limit investors to gold alone. It provides an analytical space to compare RTO + Gold with RTO + Stocks or RTO + Real Estate, enabling each investor, institution, and policymaker to align their strategies with their goals. Some may choose resilience through gold, others may pursue higher growth through equities, and others may expand through additional property ventures. The strength of Nest Quest ROI is that it makes every option transparent, comparable, and evidence-based.

The next step is to translate this framework into an operational reality. For banks and financial institutions, the question is not whether the model works in principle but how it can be implemented within existing systems to generate new product lines, strengthen depositor trust, and expand long-term stability.

Chapter 13
Implementation Strategy for Banks

This chapter describes how a universal bank implements two products, rent-to-own (RTO) and the Digital Gold Savings Account (DGSA), within the existing law and prudential practice. The design assumes no new statutes, shadow rails, or exemptions. Everything runs on supervised custody, model governance, liquidity policies and plain disclosure.

RTO is a payment allocation contract. In each cycle, a rules engine splits the customer's payment into (i) consumption (use of home), (ii) equity credit (ownership accrual), and (iii) operating costs (tax/insurance/maintenance) booked by the current ownership shares. Ownership shares are updated deterministically; hardship and exit follow pre-agreed upon mechanics.

The DGSA is a savings rail that shows two balances: grams (unit of record) and local currency (valuation). Deposits and withdrawals are in fiat currency, and conversions use published price policies and disclosed spreads. Reserves are independently attested, and redemptions are served by fiat buffers under defined service level agreements (SLAs).

Both products operate as services behind the core, with no fragile workarounds, and use tagged subledgers, event sourcing, and standard reconciliation.

Legal Placement and Jurisdiction Packs. Banks deploy jurisdictional policy packs to avoid regulatory misclassification.
Legal wrapper: RTO documented as a payment-allocation tenancy/ownership instrument (or co-ownership agreement) under local property/consumer law; DGSA documented as custody/savings (bailment or trust) with the gram as the record unit and fiat as the settlement unit.
Classification gates: If a jurisdiction classifies DGSA as a securities/custody instrument rather than a deposit product, distribution

moves under the bank/broker-dealer perimeter, disclosures are updated accordingly, and marketing is constrained to the permitted client segments. If an RTO variant is treated as unlicensed lending, the SKU is disabled or re-wrapped before going live.

Tax mapping: An internal tax rules engine maps events to local bases: DGSA gains on redemption (cost basis vs. proceeds) and RTO gains on sale/settlement. No VAT/GST on mere deposits unless the statute says so; bullion VAT exemptions applied where applicable. If a regulator mandates a mark-to-market or wealth tax, the engine adds periodic valuation/reporting without altering the customer contract.

Consumer rights overlays include cooling-off, rescission, hardship notices, dispute rights, and language requirements.

Customer Lifecycle (KYC/AML + Suitability). Onboarding tiers ensure broad and safe access:

- Tier 1 (lower limits): E-KYC + sanctions/PEP/adverse media + device binding.
- Tier 2 (moderate): Video-KYC or agent capture, income/residency proofs, and risk-based source of funds.
- Tier 3 (high): In-person verification, enhanced due diligence, and escalated monitoring.

Gold-specific compliance (where applicable): Transaction line items (weight, purity, price source, counterparty) recorded for regulatory inspection; reserve attestation proofs linked to the gram ledger.

Suitability & comprehension: Brief scenario quiz (e.g., "Hardship pauses equity credit; does it erase accrued equity?" → "No.") before activation; mis-selling triggers compliance.

Ledgers, Data, and Evidence

Subledgers (RTO): 1) Consumption receipts, 2) Equity credits, 3) Operating-cost escrows, and 4) Realized appreciation on exit.

DGSA ledgers: Gram ledger (unit of record) and valuation layer (currency equivalent). Every conversion log is a timestamp, price source, executed price, spread, fees, gram, and fiat.

Evidence controls:
- Appraisals: two independent valuations with dispersion caps; third referee if variance > threshold; sealed uploads (hash + timestamp).
- Maintenance verification: equity credit gated by upkeep proof (geo-tagged photos/videos, certified invoices, or verified inspection) for material items; failure pauses future accrual until cured (never claws back accrued equity).
- Event sourcing: All money-moving calculations are stored with inputs, outputs, and ruleset versions for replay.

Pricing & Valuation Policy (DGSA)
- Official mark: Daily cutoff; display can be intraday indicative.
- Price integrity: Primary market feed + two fallbacks, published methodology, and deterministic rounding (gram precision and legal tender currency).
- Statements: Shows grams (unchanged unless conversion) and currency equivalents (moves with the market).
- Audit: Price archives retained; reserve attestations reconciled to the gram ledger in each cycle.

Liquidity, Treasury & Redemptions
- Buffers: T+0 fiat buffer sized to the 99th percentile of daily redemptions; T+1/T+2 secondary buffer; and pre-agreed contingency lines.
- Queuing rule: If buffers are exceeded, the remaining requests are queued to the next window, disclosed in advance, and the balances continue to be marked.
- Spread governance: The treasury sets spread bands, reviews them at defined intervals, and operates an exceptions register for abnormal markets.
- Stress playbook: Price-feed outage, export/transfer ban, or bank-run scenario triggers: freeze-affected corridor, maintenance of disclosure, prioritization of unaffected buffers, and escalation to supervisors within the SLA.

Servicing & Exception Handling

RTO cycle: Engine posts split, update shares, enforce upkeep gates and issue clear statements (period + cumulative). Short pay follows the contract hierarchy, hardship flips to 'consumption plus costs for a fixed window, and automatically resumes equity credit on cure.

DGSA cycle: Engine books conversions per policy; reconcile to attestations; post redemptions within SLA, and over-buffer amounts queue transparently.

Every exception is a first-class event with an audit trail, not a manual patch.

Risk & Model Governance (Three Lines)

- First line: Runbooks, controls, metrics, and issues.
- Second line: Model validation (RTO allocation and DGSA conversion), liquidity and pricing oversight, policy attestation, and limit-setting.
- Internal audit: E-sign + effectiveness testing, vendor right to audit, and penetration of reconciliations.

Operational risk: maps failure points (pricing outage, posting error, reconciliation break, vendor downtime), assigns detective/preventive controls, and sets alert thresholds.

Disputes & Redress. Stepwise ladder: Evidence exchange → Internal adjudication (SLA) → External mediation/arbitration. Timelines are time-boxed; therefore, exits and redemptions remain competitive. All outcomes are logged, and patterns feed policy refinements.

Economics & Reporting

- DGSA revenue: Conversion spreads + disclosed custody/account fees.
- RTO revenue: Servicing fees, permitted cost recovery, and share in appreciation of principal/co-owner.
- Recognition: Per policy (execution/accrual)/
- KPI dashboards: Posting accuracy, reconciliation clean rate, conversion latency, buffer hits, complaint rate/themes, hardship entries/exits, attestation outcomes, and risk-adjusted profitability (after buffers and reconciliation costs).

Pilot → Tranche Scale

- Pilot: limited cohort + control group; full reconciliation and reporting; pre-published exit criteria (latency, buffer hits, complaint rate, attestation pass).
- Scale: Tranche gates; stop rules if metrics are breached.
- PIRs: 90/180-day reviews; change management of parameters and models; training refresh; enforced vendor remedies.

Privacy & Security. Baseline: MFA, encryption in transit/at rest, key management in HSMs, network segmentation, least-privileged access, immutable logs, continuous monitoring, third-party penetration tests, data minimization, and regional data residency, where required.

Systemic Safeguards. Cohort caps on local RTO concentration; macro dashboards for supervisors (rental yields, vacancy, price formation, hardship concurrency); staggered originations to avoid pressure on appraisers and trades; public stance against "gold hoarding"; DGSA is fiat-in/fiat-out savings, not a currency substitute.

This design is not a workaround; it is disciplined financial structuring: deterministic rules, right-sized buffers, reconciled ledgers, plain-language disclosures, and independent governance.

Note: This chapter is informational, not advice; suitability determinations belong to licensed professionals.

Chapter 14

Roadmap for Real Estate Companies

This chapter is a how-to for real estate operators who want to run Rent-to-Own (RTO), optionally paired with a bank's Digital Gold Savings Account (DGSA) rail, at scale and under supervision. It assumes no shortcuts: contracts are plain, ledgers are auditable, upkeep is enforced, residents are treated as partners, and every exit can withstand the scrutiny. The result is a business that grows on evidence rather than hype.

Banks have custody, pricing, liquidity, and regulatory capital issues. Operators hold assets, maintain valuation evidence and manage day-to-day residential relationships. The RTO turns monthly housing payments into a transparent allocation of use, equity credit, and shared operating costs, whereas the bank's DGSA rail provides a policy-neutral savings anchor between life events. This chapter describes an operator-side blueprint that enables the system to achieve predictable outcomes.

Contract Architecture (operator side): Beginning with a contract that judges can read. Each payment is divided by rule into consumption (non-recoverable use), equity credit (ownership accrual), and operating costs (taxes, insurance, and maintenance) booked by the current ownership shares. Equity accrues from the credited date, and appreciation and depreciation are allocated by shares. Upkeep thresholds are explicit: major systems and safety items must meet documented standards; otherwise, future equity credits are paused until cured (previously accrued equity never disappears). Hardship is defined ex ante as a time-boxed reversion to 'consumption plus costs' that preserves tenure and cash-flow continuity; on cure, equity resumes automatically. Exit is a settlement, not a cliff: valuation standards, cost waterfalls, and timelines are fixed in the paper; matching rights and make-whole clauses are calibrated to protect both sides without choking market timing.

Portfolio Acquisition and Underwriting. Buy the right assets; no contract design can rescue a poor foundation. Underwrite local rent-to-value ratios, stable employment basins, exposure to tax step-ups, and required hazard-coverage costs. Every purchase is stressed for three realities: flat appreciation, higher operating costs and temporary income. Pre-fund near-term capex (roofs, HVAC, safety corrections), and calendar preventative maintenance. Where coverage is required by lien or statute, document hazard coverage (peril scope, deductibles, claim timelines) before closing; where not required, quantify casualty risk and provide reserves or other mitigations appropriate to the asset class.

Pricing and Affordability Discipline. Anchor "use" pricing in observed local rent and the familiar 1/180 orientation (value ÷ 180 ≈ monthly rent) only as a starting point; then localize with comparables and cost realities. Resisting the equity split in marketing optics. If consumption is priced too low, upkeep fails and resentment follows. If equity credit is too high, the cash flow breaks at the first shock. The right price leaves both tenure and upkeep unscathed.

Operations and Maintenance Governance. Upkeep is not a suggestion; it is the backbone of the model. Publishing maintenance standards by asset classes and climate. Build a vendor network with background checks, rate cards, service-level targets, and a punch-list closeout discipline. Document everything: geo-tagged, time-stamped photos, invoices, and permits where required. Tie equity credit to the standard only prospectively, as a gate, not a trap. Residents deserve a portal that logs requests, timestamps responses, and shows status without the need to contact a call center.

Valuation and Appraisal Discipline. Fair exits require fair marks. Use rotating independent appraisers with a dispersion cap; if the first two reports disagree beyond the threshold, the third referee is bound. Prohibit "shopping" for appraisers by sealing uploads with cryptographic timestamps and immutable logs. Schedule valuation check-ins (e.g., every 24–36 months or at specified improvements), but never use mid-term marks to rewrite equity retroactively.

Resident Onboarding and Support. Treat comprehension as a prerequisite, not an afterthought. Before activation, the resident is given a one-page explainer and three scenario prompts: what happens in hardship, how upkeep gates work, and how exit is settled. Correct answers are required before signing. A brief cooling-off period allowed by law. Keep the monthly statement readable on page one (use | equity | costs | current share) with detailed pages for evidence. When hardship hits, contact quickly, trigger reversion, pause DGSA sweeps if the bank offers them, and set the path back to full-accrual. Clarity replaces conflict.

Data, Ledgers, and Privacy. Run RTO as a rule service behind the property platform. Every post is event-sourced with inputs, results, and the ruleset version, and every document is behind tamper-evident hashes. Keep the contractual state (shares, terms, cure counters) separate from the accounting (subledger balances) and operational (tickets and inspections) states. Limit access on a need-to-know basis, encrypt at rest and in transit, rotate keys, and log everything. When a regulator or arbitrator asks, it produces a ledger and evidence, not a narrative.

Liquidity and Capital Planning for Operators. Hold a real cash floor for repairs, taxes, insurance, and vacancy shocks, which is visible to management and audited quarterly. If you operate with a bank partner, avoid relying on residents' DGSA balances for your own liquidity planning; those balances are their own. Use conservative revolvers and staged capex escrows for major work. Build cadence into your cash calendar: property taxes, insurance renewals, hurricane season, freeze risks; nothing should arrive "unexpectedly."

Compliance and Conduct. Stay inside landlord-tenant law, fair housing rules, disclosure regimes, and local habitability codes. Marketing must match the reality and forbid performance promises. Standardize complaint handling with regulated timelines, escalation paths, and root cause analysis; publish remediation cycles and learn from them. Maintain an ombudsman or access to recognized mediation; you want complaints handled early and cleanly, not on the courthouse steps.

Scaling Without Breaking. Scale in tranches, not leaps. Pilot on one metro with full reconciliation: contracts, postings, evidence, hardship, and exits. Publish hard stop rules; post accuracy, appraisal dispersion, maintenance SLAs, complaint rate, and respect them. Add metros only when the supply chains (trades, materials, appraisers) are real. Train continually; the only thing worse than an untrained frontline is a trained one that you did not keep.

What to Measure? Measure what proves that you are running a system and not a story. Track posting accuracy, upkeep-gate events, response times, appraisal dispersion, hardship entries/exits and duration, exit settlement accuracy and timelines, vacancies avoided by hardship, cost-to-serve per unit, complaint themes and fixes, safety incident rates, and resident retention. These are rolled up into risk-adjusted profitability after capex and buffers. If a metric can be gamed, a second metric that captures the trick is designed.

ESG and Community Outcomes. A good RTO improves the blocks. Replace "deferred maintenance" with scheduled work; prioritize energy-efficiency upgrades that pay for themselves; contract locally, where feasible and safe; publish a short annual impact summary (units stabilized, major hazards removed, energy savings, resident retention). ESG should be a by-product of competent operations, not a brochure.

A real estate company that runs RTO well does three things relentlessly: keeps houses alive, keeps ledgers clean, and keeps promises legible. By doing so, residents become owners on a timetable that the neighborhood can believe. Banks can underwrite this with confidence. Regulators will see what you are doing for what it is: ordinary housing, made transparent, governed, and fair.

Note: This chapter is educational, not advice; suitability determinations belong to licensed professionals.

Chapter 15

The Investor Pathway & Mini Venture Capital Hubs

A venture hub ("the hub") is not a loophole; it is a governed venue for bilateral, scenario-anchored deals, cash through escrow, custody at the bank, disclosure regulators can audit, and ledgers that participants and auditors can read.

A real hub starts with people, not with paperwork. On the one hand, investors have clear aims: some want steady monthly cash, some want a fixed share of every payout reinvested automatically, and others want a time-boxed exit (five to ten years) with a transparent path grounded in reproducible mathematics, historical data, and market context. On the other hand, credit-strong earners–teachers, nurses, shop owners, and tradespeople–keep commitments and want ownership without a 30-year mortgage, without paying rent indefinitely, or (for business owners) without a long-term business loan. They are willing to pay rent costs, perhaps a bit more if those payments actually build equity.

A local financial advisor is positioned between the two. The advisor's role is not to sell a fund but to match one specific asset to one specific plan and then select a suitable pathway with which both sides can live. One such pathway is a rent-to-own structure (see Chapter 10) paired with automatic reinvestment into a bank custodial reserve, such as gold or a broad-market index (see Chapter 11) selected to match the investor's risk tolerance, volatility preferences, and liquidity needs. The reserve choice is documented in investors' Investment Policy Statement (IPS) and suitability files. In this design, payments feel like rent, but a defined share is posted to equity; investor distributions auto-sweep to the selected reserve so that the capital does not remain idle.

The operating rails are simple, transparent, auditable, and do not bend.
- The escrow holds the incoming money until the objective conditions are met (see Chapter 14).
- Bank custody holds the reinvestment reserve in a separable and verifiable account (Chapter 14 of the book).
- Conflicts and related-party transactions are disclosed and approved under the hub's policy before the funds are moved.

- The rules are locked and hashed during execution (see Chapter 13). The assumption set, rule version, and data sources are attached to the term sheet before the funds move, and any modification requires bilateral consent and is recorded in the public deal log (hashes, versions, timestamps; personally identifiable information is masked).

From this point, visibility became the norm. Monthly statements reconcile cash (not estimated). Quarterly notes compare planned versus actual inflation-adjusted using CPI-U, as specified in Methods 1.1, with plain-language drivers so that a diligent reader can verify the numbers. If anything drifts, stop rules are triggered, and remediation precedes the next intake. Trust is built through assets, plans, and ledgers.

With people and rails defined, the advisor applies them in two illustrative scenarios: educational examples focused on the participants, their preferences, and the chosen pathway.

A. Solo investor + future homeowner

Actors & preferences. *Samira* is a cautious solo investor who wants one tangible asset and directs the advisor to automatically reinvest 40% of every distribution. *Marcus* is a public school teacher with strong credit who seeks to own and move into a new home using rent-like payments that post to equity.

Pathway. The advisor pairs them on a single identified house and uses rent-to-own with automatic reinvestment of Samira's 40% into a bank custodial reserve aligned to her IPS and risk profile (e.g., gold or a broad market index). Terms are fixed in advance; cash runs on the hub's rails, and progress is reported in statements that both parties can read and understand.

Outcome window. Within the agreed window, Marcus buys out on the pre-stated formula; Samira exits with a reconciled tally of cash received and reinvested; no post-execution term changes; and any permitted amendment follows the locked-assumptions protocol.

B. Investment club + mixed loan-seekers

Actors & preferences. Eight neighbors invest together. Some want monthly cash, others elect to split and reinvest a set share of distributions, and several want a clean exit in year 10. Borrowers include *Jorge*, who runs a neighborhood print-and-ship shop and wants to own it, *and Alicia*, a nurse who wants to build on a service lot and live there.

Pathway. The advisor sets up two separate single-asset engagements on the same rails: a profit-to-equity contract for Jorge's business buyout (profit share credited toward a pre-agreed buyout formula) and a new rent-to-own path for Alicia (construction milestones, then equity-posting payments). Each investor preselects a reinvestment share and reserve type consistent with their IPS and risk preferences, and sweeps are run automatically.

Exit window. Both deals include scheduled exit windows in years 8–10. Jorge completes the buyout using the agreed formula, and Alicia purchases her home during the scheduled window. The club receives a final, reconciled tally, distribution, and reinvestment balance without changing the rules after the fact.

Other viable pathways (why was this pathway chosen?) Advisors routinely compare conventional mortgages, lease purchases, seller financing, shared equity, profit-share buyouts and municipal programs. A rent-to-own with a bank custodial reinvestment reserve is selected when (i) rent-like payments can credibly post to equity under clear upkeep and hardship rules; (ii) the investor wants automatic reinvestment matched to risk/volatility/liquidity; and (iii) both sides require frozen assumptions, escrowed flows, reconciled statements, and scheduled exits.

The parameters, including the sweep percentage, cash floors, hardship window, re-forecast cadence, and exit timing, are tuned to the case without altering the signed rulebook.

Real-world challenges, practical answers *(Educational; implementation and suitability require a licensed advisor.)*

- Appraisal variance: Rotation, dispersion caps, third opinion where needed, panel performance monitored, and sanctioned.

- Maintenance gaps: Proof-based equity credit, pre-funded capex escrow, rotated/rated inspectors, and a visible upkeep log.
- Liquidity and timing shocks: Secondary transfers (where permitted) with staged redemptions, paced construction draws, and contingency usage; rules do not change.
- Mis-selling and suitability: Plain explainer with tough-year cases, short comprehension check, and no volume-based pay.
- Model drift: Assumptions/rule versions locked and hashed; any change requires a bilateral electronic signature and public log entry.
- Disputes: Evidence exchange → bank adjudication under a published SLA → independent mediation/arbitration; tight timelines protect exits.
- Integrity stops: Data/price-feed failures, attestation variance, or the liquidity floor breaches pause intake until remedied.
- Measurement: Statements reconcile to cash; figures are inflation-adjusted using CPI-U (Methods 1.1) and reported net of all costs, fees, reserve actions, and applicable taxes; dashboards show net after all costs, not marketing yields.

A venture hub is a meeting location with specific rules. Investors keep capital working through automatic reinvestment; teachers, nurses, and local business owners buy what they use in terms of sustaining without a mortgage, perpetual rent, or long-term business debt. When the facts fit, a rent-to-own pathway with a custodial reinvestment reserve offers a clean and auditable route: equity from rent-like payments, disciplined reinvestment, and pre-set exits set in advance. Governance carries weight, and its execution makes it real.

Note: This chapter is educational, not advice; suitability determinations belong to licensed professionals.

Chapter 16

Individual Financial Management: Goals, and Ethics

Money is a system. People who learn the rules make better choices for the same income and price. You do not need more willpower; you need a clearer map to achieve your goals. This chapter turns the book's method into a short, workable plan that you can use during your worst months, not only your best.

It begins by naming two things: your aim and your limit. The objective is what you are trying to achieve over a real horizon: stability, home path, savings base, or venture capital. The limit is what you must not violate: health, family, vocation, and income that you can sustain without damage. If either is vague, the plan will drift.

Keep three views in front of you: The cash view tells you what comes in and what goes out in a normal and stressful month. The obligation view lists what you own and what you own at present value. The calendar view reminds you that hours are scarce and must include work, relationships, and recovery. A plan that ignores time fails, even when the math looks fine.

Sequence your moves. First, a cash floor sized to real bills and repairs is funded. Second, part of the recurring payment is converted into ownership only when it can be maintained under ordinary and stressful conditions. Third, preservation should be added so that the value holds its place as time passes. When the surplus is thin, stability is protected. When it thickens, it is preserved according to the schedule. Revisit the mix when reality changes.

Be aware of the rules and use them. A simple example of this is credit card transaction. Every card has two dates: a statement closing date and a payment due date. If you buy just after a statement closes and pay the full statement balance by the due date, you usually get weeks of interest-free floats, often about a month to the next close, plus another few weeks to the due date. That is a free, short loan if, and only if, you pay in full and on time. If this rule is not followed, the float disappears from the screen. Learn the rule, set calendar reminders, enable autopay for at least the statement balance before interest begins, and allow the system to work for you.

Use the engine to inform your choices. Serious decisions are modeled under identical assumptions. Read both the nominal and CPI-adjusted views. The location, policy, timing, or capital mix should be changed, and the recomputation should be monitored. Then answer the two questions that no calculator can: which values are non-negotiable, and which trade-offs will you still respect ten years from now?

Build guardrails that act without debate. If cash falls below the floor, it pauses all new commitments to spending. If ownership costs cannot be carried in stress months, slow the slope and try again in the next season. If hardship hits, use the features you planned: payment relief, clean exit math, or preservation reserve without shame. This is a plan that works as designed.

Adjustments are expected, and the process will continue. A job change, a new dependent, or a health detour; each one is a reason to re-baseline, not to abandon the design. Changing the horizon, resizing the ownership pace, or altering the savings cadence. The plan serves the household, not vice versa.

Capital is good when one understands the system it moves through. Knowledge is used to place it well. We should use our judgment to choose a path that fits our aims and limits.

Learn the rules, show the ledger, and carry out a plan that can be sustained for a hard month. Do that, and the same income will reach farther–with fewer surprises and more dignity.

Note: This chapter is educational, not advice; suitability determinations belong to licensed professionals.

Conclusion

This book aims to replace slogans with a legible flow. We formalized how rent, mortgages, RTO, and preservation products actually move value and showed how costs, taxes, and exits change the results. The aim was simple: clear inputs, transparent rules, and outputs that anyone could verify.

Nest Quest ROI is not a promise; it is a practice. It records cash in, cash out, equity, and risk with the same discipline each time, so choices can be compared on equal grounds. When facts change, the inputs are changed and recomputed accordingly. This is how good judgment is trained.

For households, the method converts long-term plans into numbers that can be lived with by households. You can see the lifetime cost of rent, mortgages, rent to own, pace of equity, and exit math. You maintain a cash floor, choose ownership only when you can maintain it, and use steady deposits to build something that holds meaning over time.

For students and educators, it functions as a laboratory. You assign parameters, replicate figures, audit methods, and grade reasoning rather than rhetoric. The lesson is portable: learn the system with respect, surface constraints, measure trade-offs, and design improvements you can defend.

For lenders and investors, the ledger is a shared and truthful record. You design or fund products, stress them under identical assumptions, and publish the parameter blocks so that others can verify your work. You adjust the location, policy, timing, or capital mix and watch the recomputation guide allocations and new venture decisions.

The same clarity applies to real estate operators and policymakers. Operators can test whether to hold, renovate, or reposition by using historical data sets and clean exit rules. Policymakers can see how taxes and regulations flow through balance sheets, set neutral rules, and reduce guesswork.

None of these proposals require the enactment of new laws. Institutional and financial infrastructure already exists. What is required is consistency: state the assumptions, model the frictions that matter, report both nominal and real outcomes, and show the ledger in strong and quiet years. Analytical judgment remains the primary mechanism.

If there is one habit to keep, it is to show the ledger. Show the allocation rule, inputs, outputs, exits, and CPI-adjusted views so that others can replicate your results. This is how trust is earned and how better designs are disseminated.

Finance is legible, resilient, and humane in nature. Implement the method in your home, classroom, practice, and shop floor. Learn the system, compare the trade-offs, and choose with clarity; then use the engine to pursue outcomes that outrun interest and resist inflation. One ledger. Shared insight. Better decisions.

NestQuestROI.com

Replication and Simulator Guide
1.   Open NestQuestROI.com
2.   Select a model (e.g., Rent-to-Own + Gold model).
3.   Enter the parameter block shown in the figure caption (rent ratio, appreciation, taxes, maintenance, vacancy, admin, and reinvestment split).
4.   Review outputs and compare them with book figures.

How to Replicate Results (Micro-Checklist)
- Compare outputs across models with identical assumptions (nominal and CPI-adjusted).
- The ruleset version/hash and parameter hash shown in the console are recorded.
- Generate the ledger: export figures/tables with series ID and date window.
- Paste or set the parameter block; note the CPI basis (CPI-U unless noted).
- Select a model (e.g., RTO, DGSA, or RTO+DGSA) and open the parameter console.

Parameter Hash (What it is and how to use it)
- If any input or ruleset changes occur, the hash changes and is used as a provenance tag.
- Include this hash in the captions to enable the exact replication of your run.
- The engine computes a short hash from the full parameter set and ruleset version.

Data Availability Statement: All parameters required to reproduce the figures appear in the captions and on NestQuestROI.com.

Methods anchors: RNIM (real adjustments on CPI-U), IRR on annual compounding, actual/actual day count, sensitivity of ±0.5–2.0 pp.

Policy Note: The DGSA does not replace sovereign currency or constrain monetary policy. It functions as an adjacent savings rail, settles in local currency with standard taxation and oversight, and broadens access to a trusted store of value without altering the currency's primacy.

Methods and Data

The internal Rate of Return (IRR) is calculated using annual effective rates with the actual/actual day-count convention. Unless otherwise noted, all units are expressed in annual percentage points (p.p.) on a Consumer Price Index for all Urban Consumers (CPI-U) basis. The Real Net Interest Margin (RNIM), formally defined in Chapter 4 and referenced throughout, is calculated as

RNIM=(Loan yield–Cost of funds–Operating cost–Expected loss)–Inflation (CPI-U)

All RNIM figures use CPI-U, unless explicitly noted. The data series presents the real and nominal values side by side. Returns are shown as IRR, with administrative, tax, and maintenance parameters detailed in the appendix tables. The assumptions are explicitly stated for each figure, without any hidden parameters. The parameter snapshots and outputs are available for download at NestQuestROI.com.

References

Official U.S. Data & Reports

- Board of Governors of the Federal Reserve System. (2025). *H.6 Money Stock Measures: Financial Accounts of the United States.* Washington, DC.
- Bureau of Economic Analysis (BEA). (2025). *NIPA Table 2.4.5U: Personal Consumption Expenditures by Type of Product.* Accessed [date]. https://apps.bea.gov/iTable/?reqid=19&step=2
- Federal Deposit Insurance Corporation (FDIC). (2025). *Quarterly Banking Profile; Q1 2025.* Washington, DC.
- Federal Deposit Insurance Corporation & Board of Governors of the Federal Reserve System. (2023). *SVB systemic risk exception communication.*
- Federal Reserve Board. (2020). *What Happened in the Money Markets in September 2019? FEDS Notes,* February 27, 2020.
- Federal Reserve. (2024). *FedNow Service: Technical Documentation and Policy Communication.*
- FRB Services. (2023). *FedNow® Service Is Now Live.* Press release, July 20, 2023.
- The Federal Reserve Bank of New York. (2025). *Markets & Policy Implementation: Repo and Reverse Repo Operations.*
- The Federal Reserve Bank of New York, (n.d.). *Large Scale Asset Purchases (LSAPs) archive.* Accessed [date].
- Internal Revenue Service (IRS). (2024). *The Tax Gap: Estimates and Methodology.*
- U.S. Bureau of Labor Statistics. (2025). *Consumer Price Index (CPI-U): Methodology and Series Tables.*
- U.S. Census Bureau. (2023). *American Community Survey, 1-Year Estimates: Table B25003 (Tenure).* Accessed [date]. https://data.census.gov/table/ACSDT1Y2023.B25003
- U.S. Census Bureau. (2025). *Homeownership and Rental Housing Statistics.*
- U.S. Department of Treasury. (2025). *Treasury General Account (TGA) Operations and Statements.*

International Standards & Regulatory Reports

- Bank for International Settlements (BIS). (2025). *BIS Quarterly Review: International Banking and Eurodollar Funding.*
- Bank for International Settlements (BIS). (2025). *Residential Property Price Statistics (Q1 2025 release).* August 28, 2025.
- Depository Trust and Clearing Corporation (DTCC). (2024). *Annual Activity and Risk Management Disclosures.*
- Financial Action Task Force (FATF). (2023). *International Standards on Combating Money Laundering and the Financing of Terrorism & Proliferation (the FATF 40 Recommendations).* Paris: FATF.
- London Bullion Market Association (LBMA). (2024). *Good Delivery Rules and Responsible Sourcing Program.*
- The Appraisal Foundation. (2024). *Uniform Standards of Professional Appraisal Practice (USPAP).* Washington, DC.

Financial Market & Industry Sources

- MSCI. (2025). *MSCI 2024 Real Estate Market Size.* New York: MSCI.

- Savills Research. (2023). *Total Global Value of Real Estate Estimated at $379.7 Trillion.* September 2023.
- S&P Dow Jones Indices. (2025). *S&P 500 Buyback Quarterly.*

Academic Literature – Microcredit & Financial Inclusion

- Banerjee, Abhijit V., et al. (2015; 2019). *Randomized Controlled Trials of Microcredit.* Various publications.
- Badruddoza, S. (2013). *Rules of the Microcredit Regulatory Authority in Bangladesh.* MPRA Paper 44637. Munich Personal RePEc Archive.
- Karlan, Dean, and Zinman, Jonathan. (2011). "Microcredit Impacts." *Review of Economics and Statistics.*
- Meager, Rachael. (2019). "Understanding the Average Impact of Microcredit Expansions: A Bayesian Hierarchical Analysis of Seven Randomized Experiments." *American Economic Journal: Applied Economics, 11*(1), 57–91.
- Roodman, David. (2012). *Due Diligence: An Impertinent Inquiry into Microfinance.* Washington, DC: Center for Global Development.

Critical Policy & Oversight – Microfinance

- Microcredit Regulatory Authority (Bangladesh). (2010). *Circular setting 27% cap (declining balance), banning upfront deductions, and grace period provisions.* The Daily Star, November 16, 2010.
- Norad. (2010). *Review Commissioned by the Norwegian Ministry of Foreign Affairs: Transfers between Grameen Bank and Grameen Kalyan.* Oslo: Norad.
- City of Detroit, Michigan. (2013). *Chapter 9 Bankruptcy Docket (Case No. 13-53846).* U.S. Bankruptcy Court, Eastern District of Michigan, USA.

Glossary

Amortization: Scheduled reduction of loan principal via periodic payments.

Asset appreciation: Change in property value over time per appreciation rate.

Basel III (CET1) : Bank capital adequacy standards (common equity tier 1).

BTFP: Bank Term Funding Program (Fed facility that lends against securities at par).

Capital gains: Increase in asset value realized at sale/recognition.

Cap rate: NOI / Property Value; a yield measure for real estate.

CPI vs. PCE: Consumer inflation measures; CPI is common for "real" conversions.

CPI-U : Consumer Price Index (All Urban Consumers)

DGSA: Digital Gold Savings Account; gram-denominated savings complementing fiat balances.

DTCC: Depository Trust and Clearing Corporation; central clearing/settlement utility.

Eurodollar: USD liabilities held outside the U.S., beyond the Fed's direct jurisdiction.

Fisher identity: Real ≈ Nominal – Inflation (small-rate approximation).

GSE: Government-sponsored enterprises that add mortgage market liquidity.

IRR : Internal Rate of Return

LTV: Loan-to-value; loan balance/property value.

Maintenance (real estate): Planned and capex outlays required to sustain rentability.

Mark-to-model: Valuation via an internal model when market prices are thin or unobservable.

Money velocity: Frequency of currency turnover in the economy.

Mortgage P&I: Principal and interest components of loan payment.

NOI: Net Operating Income = Rent – Operating Costs (before debt service and taxes).

NPV: Net Present Value

Ownership share (RTO): Evolving fraction of property attributable to each party via equity credits and appreciation allocation.

Repo market: Short-term secured inter-institution lending.

RNIM: Real Net Interest Margin

RTO: Rent-to-Own; contract that splits payments into consumption, equity credit, and shared costs.

Sharpe ratio: (Return – Risk-free)/Volatility; optional if you later add a portfolio analysis.

TGA: Treasury General Account at the Federal Reserve.

1/180 rule: Rent heuristic: monthly rent ≈ property value / 180 (varies by market).

Endnotes

[1] Brealey, Richard A., Stewart C. Myers and Allen (2020). *Principles of Corporate Finance*, 13th ed. McGraw-Hill.

[2] Federal Reserve Bank of New York (2019). "Statement Regarding Repurchase Operation(s)." (September 17–20, 2019). https://www.newyorkfed.org/markets ; The Federal Reserve Bank of New York. "Large-Scale Asset Purchases (LSAPs) Archive." https://www.newyorkfed.org/markets/programs-archive/large-scale-asset-purchases

[3] U.S. Department of Treasury. "Daily Treasury Statement." https://fiscal.treasury.gov/reports-statements/dts/

[4] U.S. Bureau of Labor Statistics. "CPI-U: U.S. City Average (Table 1)." https://www.bls.gov/news.release/cpi.t01.htm ; U.S. Bureau of Economic Analysis. "Personal Consumption Expenditures Price Index (PCE)." https://www.bea.gov/data/personal-consumption-expenditures-price-index

[5] FDIC (2025). "Quarterly Banking Profile – Q1 2025." https://www.fdic.gov/analysis/quarterly-banking-profile/

[6] U.S. Department of Treasury. "Daily Treasury Statement." https://fiscal.treasury.gov/reports-statements/dts/ ; Freddie Mac. "Primary Mortgage Market Survey (PMMS)." https://www.freddiemac.com/pmms

[7] U.S. Department of Treasury. "Daily Treasury Statement." https://fiscal.treasury.gov/reports-statements/dts/ ; U.S. Bureau of Labor Statistics. "CPI-U: U.S. City Average (Table 1)." https://www.bls.gov/news.release/cpi.t01.htm

[8] Brealey, Richard A., Stewart C. Myers and Allen (2020). *Principles of Corporate Finance*, 13th ed. McGraw-Hill. Damodaran, Aswath (2012). *Investment Valuation*, 3rd ed. Wiley.

Appendix A: Formal Ledger Proof (Sketch)

A.1 Allocation Identity. Each period's payment P_t is allocated by rule into consumption C_t, equity credit E_t, and operating costs O_t (tax, insurance, maintenance) such that $P_t = C_t + E_t + O_t$. Equity shares are updated deterministically.

A.2 Real-Accounting Consistency. Real values are obtained by CPI-U deflation of nominal cash flows; comparisons use identical deflators.

A.3 Exit Waterfall Soundness. On exit at price S, net proceeds N are S minus transaction costs; the distribution is Resident_share × N and Sponsor_share × N, plus the return of each party's equity ledger; consumption is not refunded.

A.4 Hardship Reversion Invariance. During a hardship window, equity credit pauses prospectively, and accrued equity is preserved. Upon curing, equity accruals automatically resume per contract.

A.5 Replication Tag. Each exported ledger carries a parameter hash H(parms, ruleset); any change to parameters or ruleset yields $H' \neq H$.

About the Author

Guided by the principle that perfection and creation belong to the Almighty and that designing, building, and stewardship are tests of character, Mohammed Billah is a believer, systems architect, and ethical innovator. With a background in engineering, he developed the Nest Quest ROI engine to help households, institutions, and professionals analyze rent, equity, inflation, and reinvestment using credible and reproducible methods. His work empowers users to optimize risk-adjusted returns and make informed decisions regarding financial resilience and success.

Back Cover

Nest Quest ROI was built to address challenges with practical solutions. The way it was framed and built is a method that helps curious and energetic minds learn the system, spot gaps, and design better systems.

Using the Nest Quest ROI, we studied the financial ecosystem and real estate markets. We learn how they work, identify constraints, measure trade-offs, and transform gaps into design opportunities. We built a single, reproducible ledger, tested the current and proposed models under identical assumptions, and shared the results so that everyone could compare and replicate them.

Agree with Nest Quest ROI models or outdo it. The method is the focus of this study. Keep what works. Improve what does not; that is, innovation. Replicate results, evaluate trade-offs and improve designs transparently.

www.ingramcontent.com/pod-product-compliance
Lightning Source LLC
Chambersburg PA
CBHW041005210326
41597CB00001B/16